Coldstream Guards

DRESS AND APPOINTMENTS
1658 – 1972

Charles Stadden

ALMARK PUBLISHING CO LTD, LONDON

First published — May 1973

By the same author:

THE LIFE GUARDS

ISBN 085524 110 1 (hard cover edition)
ISBN 085524 111 X (paper cover edition)

*Front cover: A Private of the Light Company of the 2nd Battalion who along
with the Light Companies of the other Guards Battalions, occupied the key
position of Hougoumont and held it against all the determined attacks the
French troops under Napoleon threw against it. A foul weather cover would
most likely have been worn but this has been omitted to show the shako detail.*

Printed in Great Britain by
Staples Printers Ltd, The Priory Press, St Albans, Herts
for the publishers, Almark Publishing Co Ltd
270 Burlington Road, New Malden
Surrey, England   KT3 4NL

Foreword

THIS the third book of the 'Dress and Appointments' series covers some of the uniform history of the Coldstream Guards from the Restoration to 1972. I have tried to make it as completely in sequence as possible, with due regard to the best utilisation of space. Both back and front views where possible are shown, and where of necessity, through lack of contemporary evidence, I have had to construct views, I have clearly stated that my interpretation is conjectural.

A work such as this would be impossible without the help of books, drawings and articles published over the years by such pioneers in research as the late Mr S. M. Milne, Mr P. W. Reynolds, Captain H. Oakes-Jones, The Reverend Percy Sumner, Mr Cecil C. P. Lawson, and many others. To them all I give my grateful thanks.

I would also like to thank those that are still with us and very actively working on research like Captain R. G. Hollies-Smith of the Parker Gallery, Mr W. Y. Carman, F.S.A., F.R.Hist.S., Major A. McKenzie Annand, T.D., Mr R. G. Harris of Southsea, Major N. P. Dawnay and the many contributors to the *Journal of the Society of Army Historical Research* without whose efforts this, or books like it, could not be produced. I would also like to extend my thanks to my very old friend Mr C. B. D. Hingle and his son Keith, who is at present serving with the 2nd Battalion Coldstream Guards, for their generous help over some queries, and last, but in no way least, Regimental Headquarters Coldstream Guards for their help and advice. The following is a bibliography of the reference sources used in preparing this book.

> *Origin and Services of the Coldstream Guards* (Col D. MacKinnon)
> *A History of the Coldstream Guards 1815–1895* (Ross of Bladensburg)
> *Coldstream Guards 1885–1914* (Col Sir J. Hall)
> *Coldstream Guards 1914–1918* (John Ross of Bladensburg)
> *Coldstream Guards 1920–1946* (Howard and Sparrow)
> *Household Brigade Magazine* (several issues)
> *Journal of the Society of Army Historical Research* (49 Volumes)
> *Military Drawings and Paintings in the Royal Collection* (Dawnay and Haswell Miller)
> *British Military Uniforms from Contemporary Pictures* (W. Y. Carman)
> P. W. Reynolds – MSS.
> *History of the Uniforms of the British Army* (C. C. P. Lawson) (5 Vols)
> *Distinction of Rank of Regimental Officers* (J.S.A.H.R.) (Dawnay)
> *Badges of Warrant and NCO's Rank in the British Army* (J.S.A.H.R.) (Dawnay)
> *Navy and Army Illustrated* (15 Volumes and 3 Volumes 1914–15)
> MSS. from Author's Collection
> Collection of Mr R. G. Harris of Southsea
> Dress Regulations 1822–1824–1846–1900.

CONTENTS

Introduction

'The Town of Coldstream, because the General did it the honour to make it the place of his residence for some time, hath given title to a small company of men whom God made instruments of Great Things; and though poor, yet honest as ever corrupt Nature produced into the World, by no dishonourable name of Coldstreamers.'

Thomas Gumble 1671.

THE Coldstream Regiment of Foot Guards trace their history and formation from two regiments of the New Model Army: Sir Arthur Hazelrigg's Regiment of five companies and Colonel Fenwick's Regiment of five companies. These ten companies were united under Colonel George Monck and were officially known as Monck's Regiment of Foot, serving with distinction at the battle of Dunbar.

Cromwell died in the autumn of 1658 and in the following year Monck, who was General Commanding in Scotland, moved his headquarters to the town of Coldstream on the Tweed. It was here the Regiment gained the title of 'Coldstreamers'.

On January 1, 1660, General Monck started from Coldstream on his historic march to London, which he reached at the beginning of February. The Coldstreamers were then used to keep order and repress the disturbances that broke out at the end of Parliamentary rule.

The end of May 1660 saw the restoration of Charles II as King of England, whereupon General Monck was created Duke of Albemarle, and his regiment commonly known as the Coldstreamers, were inspected by the King on his triumphant entry into London.

On February 14, 1661 (1660 old calendar), Monck's Regiment of Foot were mustered on Tower Hill and ordered to lay down their arms and disband, then were immediately ordered to take them up in the name of the King as the Second Regiment of Foot Guards, this they refused to do, saying they were second to none. They were then ordered to take up their arms as the Lord General's Regiment of Foot Guards. From that moment the Regiment became personal Guards to the Sovereign of the Realm. In the following years the Regiment served as marines with the Fleet, as well as sending a detachment of fifty men to North America.

Monck the Duke of Albemarle died in April 1670 and the Lord General's Regiment was conferred upon the Earl of Craven, it was from this time the name of the regiment was officially known as the Coldstream Regiment of Foot Guards.

In 1678 the Regiment served in Flanders and in 1685 took part in the battle of Sedgemoor, which ended the Monmouth Rebellion. The Regiment sent a detachment of two officers and 130 other ranks to Tangier in 1680 to form part of the King's Battalion stationed there. After 1688 and William and Mary's accession to the throne the Regiment embarked for Flanders and was engaged in the battle of Walcourt, 1689, the battle of Landen in the campaign of 1693, and the siege of Namur, 1695. After several major engagements the Peace of Ryswick was signed and the 1st Battalion came home in November 1697. 'Namur 1695' becoming their second battle honour.

In July 1702, six companies of the Coldstream were included in a composite battalion of Guards that were sent to Cadiz and Vigo. In July 1704, 400 men of the Coldstream and 200 of the 1st Guards, formed a composite Guards battalion for service in Portugal, and they also saw service at Gibraltar and Spain.

A renewal of the war in Flanders, again saw the Regiment on active service, where they took part in the battles of Oudenarde 1708 and Malplaquet 1709. From 1715 to 1742 the Regiment enjoyed their first long spell of peace, but this was broken by the dispatch of seven companies to Spain, which culminated in the surrender of Vigo. May 1742, King George II being on the throne, the 1st Battalion with the two other Guards battalions, embarked for service again in Flanders in support of the cause of Maria Theresa and were present at the battle of Dettingen, but this time they were in the rearguard. This battle was notable as being the last occasion on which a King of England has personally commanded an army in the field.

The Regiment took a distinguished part in the battle of Fontenoy, on its field the Coldstream left 250 dead and wounded. This battle though technically a defeat, remains a monument to the value of discipline and fire control of the British Army.

The 2nd Battalion proceeded to Flushing in May 1747 and joined the Allied Army till after the peace of Aix-la-Chapelle 1749. In July 1760 the 2nd Battalion went to Germany with the other two Guards battalions and were engaged in the campaigns under Prince Ferdinand of Brunswick and the Marquis of Granby. They took a distinguished part in the battle of Wilhelmsthal and at the Castle of Amoneberg, which proved to be the final engagement of the campaign. The Battalion returned home in 1763. In 1776 owing to the outbreak of the War of Independence in the American Colonies, a composite battalion was formed from the three regiments of Guards under the command of Colonel Mathew of the Coldstream. The Coldstream contingent consisted of 307 men of all ranks. Early in 1777 the battalion was formed into two battalions, with Colonel Mathew as Brigadier. The battalions were engaged in operations throughout the war and returned home after the capitulation of Lord Cornwallis at Yorktown to a superior American force of 20,000 men of whom 7,000 were French.

Owing to the crisis of the Revolution in France in 1793, and the murder of Louis XVI of France, Britain joined the confederacy against the Republican Government, and once more the Coldstream 1st Battalion joined the 1st Battalions of the other two Guards regiments to form a Guards brigade. This consisted of four battalions, the fourth being made up from the Grenadier companies of the three regiments, and these embarked for the Continent. The Brigade took a distinguished part in the subsequent campaigns, the Siege of Valenciennes and at Lincelles, and in the several small engagements and skirmishes of more or less importance. The Coldstream arrived home in May 1795. In August 1799 the 1st Battalion Coldstream and 1st Battalion 3rd Guards were brigaded under General Burrard for service in Holland under Sir Ralph Abercrombie. They took part in the campaign that ended with the Battle of Egmont-op-Zee.

The 1st Battalion was engaged in the expedition against Vigo and from there sailed to join the Army under Sir Ralph Abercrombie in Egypt, taking part in the operations that ended with the surrender of the French Army of Occupation in Cairo. The Regiment was awarded the distinctive badge of the Sphinx superscribed, 'Egypt', for their conspicuous services in the campaign that blighted Napoleon's dream of Oriental conquest. The Battalion returned home after a short stay in Malta.

The 1st Battalion was sent with a British force to Bremen in 1805, but returned home in February 1806. But they were again in 1807 landed on the Danish coast and took part in the investment of Copenhagen. The 1st Battalion, in the same brigade, were sent to Portugal in January 1809 to the Army under Sir Arthur Wellesley. They served at the Passage of the Douro, capture of Oporto and the battle of Talavera, as well as the following campaigns of 1810–14 including the sieges of Ciudad Rodrigo, Badajos, Burgos and San Sebastian, the battles of Fuentes d'Onoro, Salamanca, Vittoria, Pyrenees, Bidassoa, Nive Nivelle and the investment of Bayonne. The 2nd Battalion were in the Walcheren Expedition (Flank companies) and the battalion companies of the same battalion served under General Graham at Cadiz and fought at the battle of Barrosa. After this the companies along with those of the other regiments of Guards, were sent home. In 1813 six companies of the 2nd Battalion proceeded to Holland and took part in the unsuccessful but gallant assault on Bergen-op-Zoom. These companies remained in garrison in Brussels and later at Ath.

When Napoleon returned to France from Elba, the companies at Ath were reinforced from home by four companies and the Headquarters of the 2nd Battalion, which now made the 2nd Battalion complete. The battalion joined the 2nd Guards Brigade which also included the 2nd Battalion, 3rd Guards, under Major-General Byng.

At Quatre Bras the Coldstream acted in support of the 1st Guards Brigade and on June 18 at Waterloo the 2nd Brigade of Guards were posted on the ridge above Hougoumont on the right of the 1st Guards Brigade under Maitland (2nd and 3rd Battalions 1st Guards). The four Light Companies from the four battalions in the brigades, occupied and defended the farm of Hougoumont, the key to the British position, throughout that memorable day. The story of Waterloo and the Coldstream part in it is so well known there is no need to retell it here.

The 2nd Battalion took part in the subsequent occupation of Paris, remaining in France until the summer of 1816. The 1st Battalion went to Portugal in 1827–28, the 2nd to Canada during the troubles of 1838–42.

In 1831, by the sanction of King William IV, the Coldstream adopted the bearskin cap that had previously only been worn by the grenadier companies of the Regiment. The distinction of a red plume (cut feathers for officers and senior NCOs) and horse hair for the men, was worn on the right side.

The 1st Battalion embarked for the Crimea in 1854 and took a distinguished part in the campaign at the battles of Alma, Inkerman and Sevastopol. The Treaty of Paris brought peace on March 30 1856 and the 1st Battalion returned to England in June of that year. The Victoria Cross was instituted early in 1856 and four Coldstreamers were awarded this coveted decoration; Brevet majors Goodlake and Conolly and privates Strong and Stanlack.

From 1856 to 1882 the Regiment was not called for active service, but on August 1 1882 the 2nd Battalion embarked from Ireland to join the Guards Brigade for service in Egypt against the rebels under Arabi Pasha. The brigade consisted of the 2nd Battalion Grenadiers and 1st Battalion Scots Guards which was commanded by Major-General HRH the Duke of Connaught, KG, the arrival of the 2nd Coldstream completing the brigade. The campaign ended after the battle of Tel-el-Kebir and the 2nd Battalion returned home on November 16. Again in 1884 the Coldstream sent a detachment of ninety-two men of all ranks to join the Camel Corps under Lieutenant-Colonel the Honourable E. Boscawen, Coldstream Guards.

Early in 1885 the 1st Battalion embarked for the Suakin Campaign and took part in the actions at Hashin and were in support at Tofrek, the battalion returned home in September. From 1885 to 1897 the Regiment was left undisturbed by operations or administrative change, but in the latter year, 1897, Parliament sanctioned the addition of a 3rd Battalion to the Regiment and colours were presented to the new battalion by Queen Victoria at Aldershot in July 1898.

In 1899 on the outbreak of the Boer War, the 2nd Battalion left for South Africa, the 1st Battalion also embarked from Gibraltar for the same destination. Both battalions were encamped near the Orange River Station by November, and both battalions played a very distinguished part in the campaigns that followed, and on the conclusion of peace in May 1902, both battalions came home arriving at Aldershot in October 1902.

On September 29 1906 the 3rd Battalion left England for Egypt, and returned to England in March 1911. In August 1914 on the outbreak of war with Germany, the Coldstream was immediately involved and took part in the Mons Retreat, the Marne, Aisne and Ypres 1914–15 and in the following campaigns and battles that culminated in the Armistice of 1918. This war was notable because for the first time in their history the Coldstream battalions were composed, from 1915 onwards, mainly of short service officers and men who had joined for the duration of the war, and from 1918, by conscripts.

In recognition of the gallantry of the Brigade of Guards in the 1914–18 War, the King on November 22 1918 ordered that in future the title Guardsman should be used instead of Private as heretofore. The Coldstream were in the Army of Occupation and on February 18 1919 the 4th (Pioneer) Battalion was disbanded.

Full Dress was re-introduced in 1922, having been discontinued in 1914 on the outbreak of war.

The 3rd Battalion in 1922–23 served in the Army of the Black Sea at Constantinople. The 2nd Battalion went to the Far East as part of the Shanghai Defence Force 1927–28, and the 1st Battalion spent a two-year tour in Egypt and the Sudan 1932–33.

In 1936 all three Battalions of the Regiment received new Colours from HM King Edward VIII, and in the autumn of the same year the 3rd Battalion was engaged in suppressing the disorders in Palestine.

On the outbreak of World War 2 in 1939 the 1st and 2nd Battalions were by no means fully equipped, in common with the rest of the Army, but were ready to take the field with the BEF in France. In the following six years the Coldstream were engaged in the fighting in many parts of the world, France, 1939–40, Egypt 1939–42, North Africa 1942, Italy 1943–45, Normandy to the Baltic 1944–45. The battles were too numerous to list here in this brief account of the regimental history of this famous regiment. During this war they served both as infantry and in Armoured Battalions in Sherman and Churchill tanks, again amply confirming their motto that they are 'second to none'.

After the German surrender the Guards Division gave up its armour at a ceremonial parade attended by Field Marshal Montgomery and was part of the Army of Occupation once again as an Infantry Division in the Cologne area.

The 5th Battalion was disbanded in October 1945, and the 3rd Battalion was sent to the Middle East as part of the 1st Guards Brigade which had been intended for the Far Eastern Theatre of the War, but the early collapse of the Japanese made this unnecessary.

The 4th Battalion was disbanded in 1946 and also the Coldstream Training Battalion, whose personnel were distributed between the newly formed 1st and 2nd Guards Training Battalions.

The 2nd Battalion arrived home in September 1946 from Trieste where it had been since the German surrender in Italy in May 1945.

In the Autumn of 1946 the Guards Division was broken up and the 1st Battalion came home and was stationed at Pirbright. Volunteers from the Brigade of Guards in 1947, were trained as parachute troops. The Coldstream element was five Officers and 150 other ranks. This Guards contingent finally became the 16th Guards Independent Parachute Company.

Full Dress was reintroduced in the summer of 1948, but the old Guard Order of Slade-Wallace equipment and folded cape gave way to waist-belt and bayonet frog only.

The 2nd Battalion sailed on September 5 1948 with the 2nd Guards Brigade for Malaya and took part in the operations against the Communists in Northern Malaya.

Since then the Coldstream battalions have been engaged in several internal security duties such as Aden, and more recently the troubles in Northern Ireland. The Battalions are also stationed in Germany and train in NATO countries in conjunction with other NATO units.

The past history of this very famous and distinguished Guards Regiment of well over three centuries, is a story of which the Coldstreamers can be proud, a record that is truly 'second to none'.

This photograph of the Corps of Drums of the 1st Coldstream, was taken at Chelsea Barracks. The Drum Major's dress is as described in Fig 47. The dress of the drummers had not basically changed since the 1860s. The tenor drum, a larger type of side drum, was at this time becoming a popular addition to the Corps of Drums of the infantry, and can be seen immediately behind the Drum Major. The fife cases were worn on the right side.

The Uniforms

Although the Coldstream Guards trace their descent from 1650, as stated in the Introduction, it was not until February 14 Saint Valentine's Day 1661 (1660 old calendar) that they became Foot Guards, so it seems in order to start this history of their dress and appointments at this period.

The musketeer wears a black felt hat, with a red feather, not too high in the crown, a large fall-down linen collar over a red coat, the sleeves of which had slits fastened by white metal buttons, the cuffs were of white linen. Breeches and stockings were red with green ribbon garters. Sometimes a buff leather jerkin was worn over the coat. The bandolier has the twelve 'Apostles' or wooden cartridge cases, also, attached to the bandolier was the priming flask and leather bullet bag, and when not in use, the slow match. Over the right shoulder is the sword-belt, the sword having a steel hilt. The musketeer was armed with a matchlock and carried a rest for the heavy weapon. (The rest appears to have gradually fallen into disuse during the Civil War, though it is possible it lingered on for a while after, as it is shown in some prints and illustrations.)

The Pikeman wears the steel 'Pott' helmet, his armour consists of back and breast plates and tassets; steel thigh armour. These last were very soon discarded after the Restoration. A white fall-down linen collar, a buff leather jerkin and leather gauntlet gloves. A white sash with green fringes. Red breeches and stockings with green ribbons. The shoes for both men were of a grey buff colour with green bows. He was armed with a steel hilted sword and a 16 foot pike. A red feather may have been worn in the helmet.

Fig 2: Officers of The Lord General's Regiment of Foot Guards, 1664

Nothing much is known of the dress of the officers of the Coldstream at this time, except in a general way for the Army, such as it was at this period. It seemed that officers in general followed closely civilian fashion of the time. The coat was now getting longer and followed the Continental style. Hollar's sketches of Tangier give us some idea of the officers' style of uniform but as these were an early attempt at a kind of tropical dress, they are no help as regards colouring, but the cut etc, did follow fashion.

There is a contemporary oil painting at Hampton Court of Charles II leaving Holland in June 1660 and the figures of the foreground troops are thought to be of the King's Foot Guards (Grenadier Guards) and one officer wears a blue coat with red facings, although he could be a Dutch officer. Another has a yellow or gold embroidered coat with blue breeches.

The coats of the Coldstreams may have been of crimson cloth laced and embroidered in gold, with crimson breeches and stockings, the ribbon garters possibly of green silk. It was not until a few years later that the coat was more waisted and a sash was worn round the waist. I have included this drawing because of its interest value and to show the difference between this period and the officers shown in Fig 7. It must however be regarded as conjectural.

Fig 3: Pikeman, Coldstream Regiment of Foot Guards, *c.* 1670

The dress of the Pikemen in the Coldstreams as shown in the drawing above, consists of a steel 'Pott' or helmet with scaled ear pieces. Steel back and breast plates. Green coat with red cuffs (Pikemen had the coat the same colour as the facings of the Regiment, the Musketeers having red coats with green facings). The buttons possibly of white metal. The sword suspended from a buff leather shoulder-belt. Red breeches and stockings, and white garter ribbons. White sash with green fringes. White bows on the shoes. The pike 16 feet long.

The detail is from an old drill manuscript for the Pikes, 'Draw your sword and order your pike'.

The number of Pikes in a battalion of infantry at this time was about a third of the total strength. This was gradually reduced, and by the time of the outbreak of the War of the Spanish Succession, they do not seem to have been used at all on active service, as no mention of them is recorded. They were still used, evidently for ceremonial occasions, as the Colours taken from the French after the battle of Blenheim were carried through London by the Pikes of the Foot Guards.

The dress detail for this drawing, was taken from contemporary engravings of the funeral of General George Monck, Duke of Albemarle, who died in January 1670. Both the Drum Major and Drummers are shown, as well as the Fifers (the drums are draped, and the fifes have banners attached to the tube, both of these items have General Monck's Coat of Arms embroidered thereon). It is reasonable to assume that these figures belong to Monck's own Regiment, The Coldstream, as they would certainly be there. The engravings were not coloured, so it is only possible to surmise what the colouring could be, taking into account the information known about the Coldstream themselves, and the Army as such, at that time. As drummers seemed to have followed the custom of the Pikes in having their coats of the facing colour, it is possible that these could be green with red cuffs, red stockings and breeches. The ribbons and bows could be yellow or green. The head-dress black bound possibly in silver lace. The drum major's dress could be similar, the sash crimson, and the waistcoat red with white shirt sleeves.

Fig 5: Grenadier of the Coldstream Regiment of Foot Guards, *c.* 1678

An order dated May 19 1677, directed that two soldiers from each company of the Foot Guards were to be trained and exercised by a Captain Charles Lloyd for the duty of Grenadiers. This was the first reference to forming and training men as grenadiers, by 1678 a Grenadier Company had been added to the Regiment.

Their head-dress was a departure from the normal hat, owing possibly, to the necessity of having to sling and carry their firelocks across their backs when using the grenade. The cap was similar to the sailors cap of the time, with the body of the cap consisting of a bag made of red cloth, bound round the base with green cloth, and had a green cloth raised front, on which was the Royal Cypher and Crown. The green cloth base and edge of the raised front was bound in yellow lace, the cap was lined in green with a green tassel.

The coat was of red cloth with yellow lace and green edges. Breeches and stockings of red with possibly yellow ribbons at the knee.

The equipment worn consisted of brown leather belts; a shoulder-belt for the grenade pouch, a frog to carry the hammer-headed hatchet and waist-belt with a large frog to carry the brass hilted sword. A cartouche box on a girdle was carried plus a plug bayonet in a small frog carried on the left front of the waist-belt. The firelock was a snaphaunce musket with a leather sling attached.

The Grenadiers were really, in their day, similar to modern commandos, and had the same glamour. Their job was to soften up the defence with their grenades and clear away obstacles using their hatchets.

Fig 6: Musketeer, *c.* 1675 and Grenadier, 1685 of the Coldstream Regiment of Foot Guards

The dress of the Musketeer at this period, was a black felt hat bound in yellow lace, the coat was of red cloth and the facings possibly green. In a return dated 1684 for the Coldstreams, it stated, 'Red coats lined green, red stockings and breeches'. This would indicate that the Regiment had green facings right up to the issue of the new clothing for the Coronation of James II, when the facings were changed to blue. (Sandford in his description of the Coronation mentions 'new Clothes' for the Coldstream.)

In the book Records and Badges of the British Army, *by Chichester and Short, in the section devoted to the Coldstream Guards, they state that the facings were changed in 1670, this may be a mistake due to the confusion over a Wardrobe Warrant dated April 17 1669, authorizing the issue of new Colours to the Regiment of blue, '48 ells of blue sarsenet, 22 ells of crimson and 20 ells of white'. These to replace the existing twelve Colours.*

The breeches of red broad cloth, with red worsted stockings, the ribbons below the knee and bows on the shoes possibly yellow. The equipment consisted of a 'Collar of Bandoliers', sword in a sword-belt over the right shoulder, and a snaphaunce musket with the barrel 3 feet 8 inches in length, having no strap or sling. The Musketeers in 1685 carried the sword in a waist-belt, instead of in a shoulder-belt as before. They still carried the 'Collar of Bandoliers'. mentioned above. Their facings now being blue. Bayonets were issued to the Musketeers in 1686. It must be stressed that uniform detail at this time is very scarce, so it cannot have been described in any great detail regimentally, though the general appearance of the soldier was well known.

The detail for the Grenadier is taken from Sandford's description of the 'Coronation of James II'. According to this, Sandford states 'The Private soldiers were all new clothed in coats of red broad cloth lined and faced in blew', see above. The grenadier cap was lined and faced with blue and laced in yellow, the front had the King's Cypher and Crown embroidered (Sandford mentions the fronts of these caps 'were large and high'). The coat was of red cloth faced and lined in blue and the lace possibly of yellow worsted with tufted ends. Red breeches and stockings. The ribbons and bows possibly yellow. The equipment was 'Granado Pouch, Cartouch box, Bionet and Hammer hatchet, Sword and Long Carbine strapt'.

Fig 7 : Officers of the Coldstream Regiment of Foot Guards, *c.* 1680

Information on the dress of the Army at this period is very scarce, but we are fortunate in having two paintings of the Coldstream Guards in existence, one belongs to the Duke of Roxburghe, and a full description of this picture was featured in an article, both in the Journal of the Society of Army Historical Research *and the* Household Brigade Magazine, *by Major P. R. Adair of the Coldstream Guards. The other picture is at Berkeley Castle. Both pictures show the Regiment on parade, possibly Guard Mounting, on the Horse Guards Parade, the first about 1680 and the latter 1674.*

My illustration is based on these pictures. The officers' head-dress is black with silver lace binding, both officers have full wigs, white lace cravats, and shirt sleeves. The coat is of a brownish/crimson colour and is quite plain, the cuffs and linings are of the same colour as the rest of the coat. Breeches and stockings are also of the same colour. The sword-belt is of a buff colour, edged with gold lace. A crimson sash with silver tasselled ends is worn round the waist. The buttons appear to be of gold or gilt. The shoes were black with white bows. The officers are armed with a full length pike of 16 feet.

Major Adair is of the opinion that this dress may have been an undress uniform of the officers.

Fig 8: Officers of The Coldstream Regiment of Foot Guards, *c.* 1705–1720

Details of the officers' dress at this period is difficult to find, as no regulation existed and the only sources available to us are by pictures, portraits and references to the dress in orders, clothing bills, etc, issued at that time. From the existing evidence, it seemed that there was no uniformity of dress in general for the officers of the Army, and even in the different ranks, was not marked in their dress, as both senior and junior officers appeared to have similar amounts of gold or silver lace on their coats and appointments.

As to the dress of the officers of the Guards we do have the Blenheim Tapestries, and the illustration is based on this and other references mentioned before. The description for the Coldstream as follows must be regarded as conjecture but I believe is a fair idea of the dress of this particular period.

Head-dress is a black tricorne, laced in gold, with black bow and tie in gold lace with gold button. A full wig was worn of a natural colour. The coat of scarlet cloth, faced blue; blue cuffs and linings (some pictures show scarlet cuffs). All lace gold, laced down the seams; buttons possibly of the embroidered type in gold. Crimson silk sash with gold fringes. Gilt hilt sword, buff waistbelt worn under sash, with buff frog, black scabbard gilt mounts. Blue breeches and white stockings, black shoes with gilt buckles. Officers carried the espontoon, or short pike.

The 1st Battalion, The Coldstream Regiment of Foot Guards in conjunction with two battalions of the 1st Guards, the 1st Battalion Scots Regiment of Foot Guards and a battalion of Dutch Guards stormed the outlying defences of the city of Namur in 1695. The colour illustration shows Grenadiers of the Grenadier Company, 1st Battalion The Coldstream Regiment of Foot Guards breaking down the palisades. The officer carries the Lieutenant-Colonel's colour and in the background can be seen the Musketeers of the Battalion companies advancing through the smoke. The uniforms shown here are fully described on pages 14 and 15. This was the first instance of all three Guards Regiments being brigaded together in battle.

Fig 9: Private Man of the Battalion Company and Grenadiers of The Coldstream Regiment of Foot Guards, 1708–1720

Information on the dress of the Army at this period is to say the least, rather scarce and pictorial evidence is even scarcer. We get many references in the clothing returns, bills, advertisements for deserters, etc, but all these are rather vague as to precise regimental detail. The drawing is based on these and the Blenheim Tapestries and pictures of the period. The description of the dress is as follows: The Private Man has the black tricorne, bound in yellow lace, (an advertisement for a deserter in 1712 states 'Deserter with all his regimental cloathing being red lined blue and brass buttons. The waistcoat lined with yellow, a hat with yellow worsted lace'). The wearing of yellow lace on the coats of the rank and file of the Coldstream Regiment of Foot Guards seems to have been abolished sometime between 1720 and 1742, and white lace loops adopted.

The Grenadiers' cap had a blue front and 'little flap', a yellow embroidered crown with a crimson cap and white embroidered star, possibly the Garter Star, white scrolls, the whole laced in yellow lace round the edge of the front. The little flap edged in yellow lace, the design in white embroidery is not clear, but could be a grenade in the centre. Back of the cap red, laced in yellow lace, the back flap blue, with what appears to be crossed muskets embroidered in white. The shirts and cravats white cotton. Hair natural and tied in a queue. The coats the same for all, red cloth with a blue cape (collar) cuffs and linings, all lace plain yellow, the buttons brass. The equipment of brown leather, brass buckles, black pouch with a brass star badge. White gaiters or long stockings pulled up over the knee were worn. Black garter straps and shoes: these had the high tongues of the period and fastening with buckles.

Fig 10: Pioneer and Private Man of the Battalion Company, 1742–1750

The detail for the pioneer is taken from Hogarth's picture of the 'March of the Guards to Finchley'. Though there are several references to pioneers at this period, in orders, clothing returns, etc, pictorial evidence is very scarce, so although no great reliance can be placed on Hogarth's regimental detail in his pictures, he was an artist concerned in depicting an over-all view of life as it was in his time, and did not concern himself with the very small details of regimental dress. An example of this is his rendering of the design upon the grenadier caps of the Guards, which we know by existing evidence is incorrect, even so, many artists both past and present, British and foreign, lacking the real background knowledge of uniform, have copied Hogarth's rendering of the design. But in the general appearance of the soldier of his time, his work is invaluable.

Coupled with Hogarth's picture and the many regimental orders, clothing returns, bills, etc, to pioneers, I have endeavoured to reconstruct the possible dress and equipment of the pioneer.

The head-dress is red cloth, similar to the type of cap as worn by sailors of this period, a kind of bag the end of which was a white tassel, a blue cloth turn-up, on which embroidered in white, a mattock and saw, white scroll embroidery at the sides and back. Hair is natural and appears to be turned up under the cap. The coat is the normal rank and file pattern, faced and laced exactly as described below for the Private Man. The coat is shown buttoned across in this case. The breeches and gaiters as for the private. The equipment is the same as the private, and has a sword of normal design. A buff leather apron hooked up on the left side.

With the Private Man we are on much firmer ground as regards the dress, as we have 'A Representation of the Cloathing of His Majesty's Household and all the Forces upon the Establishments of Great Britain and Ireland' commonly

(continued on page 22)

The Grenadier Company of the 1st Battalion in Bivouac, circa 1750. While one man prepares the meal, another collects wood for the fire, others are pitching the tents. Two officers are checking the area, and beyond them can be seen a battalion man being posted as sentry. The two grenadiers sitting by the fire sharing rations will be possibly the first relief for picket duty. The dress of the officers and men are fully described on pages 23, 26 and 27.

In May 1742 the 1st Battalion embarked at Woolwich with two other Guards battalions for service in Flanders in support of the cause of Maria Theresa and took part in the battles of Dettingen, 1743 and Fontenoy, 1745. But owing to the rebellion of Bonnie Prince Charlie, they returned home with the bulk of the British Army, and arrived at the Tower of London in September 1745. The Battalion then remained in Britain for several years.

The 2nd Battalion on a Field Day in Hyde Park circa 1790. The battalion is drawn up in parade formation awaiting the march back to barracks. The Drum-Major, at right, giving orders to the Drummer and Fifer of the Battalion Company has a silver-laced hat as is the lacing on his coat. The bastion loops are feathered in blue round the edges and have silver tassels. The drummer and fifer are dressed in similar fashion but with white lacing and blue fleur-de-lis plain white lace on the cuffs, lapels and loops of the coat. The dress of the officers and men is fully covered in the text.

These Field Days seem to have been a popular form of amusement for the population of London, but if the contemporary cartoons of the day, notably those by Rowlandson and Gillray, are to be believed this was quite a hazardous form of sport and people were not infrequently hurt during full-scale demonstrations.

called The Cloathing Book. *This was the first serious effort to standardize and record the dress of the Army. It consisted of a series of hand-coloured engraved plates, showing men of all the regiments of Horse, Dragoons and Foot as well as Pensioners and Yeoman of the Guard.*

The infantry plates show only the Battalion Companies dress of the Guards, Fusiliers, and Line Infantry. No grenadiers are illustrated. The detail of the figure in the illustration is from the plate devoted to the 2nd Guards.

The head-dress is the black tricorne, with lace round the top in plain white tape lace. Black bow and white worsted tie and button. Hair is natural and tied in a queue. The coat was of red cloth, with blue lapels, cuffs and linings. The coat was large, the skirts falling to the knee. The lapels were laced around the edges and down the front and along the edge of the slit at the back, in plain white lace; seven buttonhole loops on each lapel and two below in front, three at the back, top one above the slit, the other two each side below, all in the same plain white lace. The slash pockets were laced down to the skirt edge, and had four lace loops on each side.

The breeches were of blue cloth, and the gaiters were white with black buttons; shoes black. All buttons were of pewter.

The equipment was a broad buff leather belt for the pouch having three brass buckles, one on the breast and two each side above the pouch, on the end of the belt was attached the brush and picker for cleaning the vent and pan of the musket. The pouch was black leather with no ornament. The pouch-belt was worn under the waist-belt in front, but over it at the back. The waist-belt was also of buff leather, with a brass buckle, suspended by a buff leather double frog was the brass hilted sword and bayonet, both in black scabbards with brass mounts.

Fig 11 : Officers of the Battalion and Grenadier Companies, 1742–1751

Owing to the lack of any regulations at this time regarding the dress of the officers, the only evidence is with contemporary portraits, paintings and water-colours, also prints, etc, of which there is quite a number. From these I have contrived to piece together a reasonable assumption of the dress of the officers of the Coldstream Guards at this period, so the following details and the illustration must be regarded as conjectural.

The head-dress for the battalion company officer was the black tricorne, laced in gold, with a gold lace tie. (Grenadier officers also wore this hat, on occasions when the Grenadier cap was not worn.) The Grenadier cap, blue front, red flap, gold and silver thread.

The hair was usually powdered and tied in a pig-tail with black ribbons. The Grenadier officers when wearing the Grenadier cap, wore their hair plaited and turned up under the cap.

The shirt frill was white and having lace at the throat and the wrists. The gorget was gilt with the Royal Arms engraved, and fastened by blue ribbons and rosettes, these items were the same for both officers.

The coat was the full dress state coat (the frock was plainer and was said for the Coldstream to be of blue cloth, with a small amount of gold lace), with blue lapels, cuffs and linings, the whole heavily laced with gold, gold buttons; gold and crimson aiguillettes on the right shoulder. The back of the coat was laced at the waist above the slit of the skirts, with one loop and two each side of the slit underneath, down each side of the slit, along each edge and along the bottom of the skirts was gold lace about ¾ inch wide. There did not seem at this time any marked difference between the rank of the officers, or between the regiments of Guards, in the dress of this period. The coat of the Grenadier officer was similar in all respects to the battalion officer.

The waistcoats of both officers were of buff cloth, laced in gold. In the year 1749 it was ordered that the officers of the Coldstream were to wear buff breeches as well as buff waistcoats.

A crimson silk sash was worn over the right shoulder and tied on the left hip, while the Grenadier officer wears his round the waist, this was ordered on April 25, 1748 in a brigade order, that Grenadier officers of all Guards regiments were to wear their sashes in this manner.

The battalion officer is shown in breeches and stockings and carrying a gold headed cane, he is on duty though, as he is wearing his gorget. On parade he would be wearing white spatterdashes like the Grenadier; he would also be armed with an espontoon. Grenadier officers carried a fusil and bayonet, for this reason they also wore a buff shoulder belt, with gilt buckles, to carry the pouch which was covered in velvet, edged in gold lace and having the Royal Cypher embroidered in the centre.

The swords of both officers were the same, having a gilt hilt with ivory grip, gold and crimson sword knot, black scabbard with gilt tip. These were suspended from a buff waist-belt with a gilt buckle, not seen on the Grenadier officer in the illustration.

Fig 11

2nd Battalion, Coldstream Regiment of Foot Guards on the morning of June 18, 1815. The colour plate shows men of the Grenadier and Battalion companies taking up position for the Battle of Waterloo. All ranks are wearing the foul weather oilskin covers over their shakos, not surprising after the night of storm and rain that preceded the actual battle. In this engagement the 2nd Battalion was brigaded with the 2nd Battalion of the 3rd Guards and known as 2nd Guards Brigade under the command of Major-General Byng. The 1st Guards Brigade was formed from the 1st and 2nd Battalions of the 1st Guards. The dress of all ranks is fully described in the text.

In 1831 a submission was made to the Government of the time that the Coldstream and 3rd Guards, should be renamed the Coldstream Fusilier Regiment of Foot Guards and the 3rd Fusilier Regiment of Foot Guards; the uniform of both regiments to be as Fusiliers.

The outcome of this was that the bearskin cap was adopted by both regiments, but the Coldstream did not take kindly to the Fusilier title, and so remained Coldstream Guards.

It was intended that the plumes should be white and worn on the left, but the Coldstream took a scarlet cut feather and wore it on the right side of the bearskin cap.

The colour plate shows different ranks of the Regiment after the adoption of the bearskin cap. On the extreme left is a Band Sergeant and a Bandsman, tunic lace is all gold and the loops across the breast have gold tassels at each end. Silver embroidered Garter Stars are worn on the collar and skirt ornaments. The officers dress is fully described on page 51.

The Colour Sergeant at right has lace and epaulettes of gold with silver embroidered Garter Stars on the collar patches.

The Private has lace and epaulettes of white worsted, and a plain blue collar with white embroidered Garter Stars.

Fig 12 : Private, Guard Order, 1747, Corporal Marching Order 1751, Grenadier Company, Coldstream Regiment of Foot Guards

The detail for this private is taken from a contemporary water-colour by Thomas Sandby featured in an article by the late Reverend Percy Sumner, in the Journal of the Society of Army Historical Research, *Volume 27.*

The head-dress is the Grenadier mitre cap, having a blue front which is embroidered at the top with a Crown in the full colour, the Garter Star, the star in white thread, the garter in blue edged yellow with yellow lettering, red cross in the centre; white scroll embroidery each side. The little 'flap' is blue (soon to be changed to red) having the motto 'NEC ASPERA TERRENT' round the top, and the white Horse of Hanover underneath. The back of the cap was of red cloth embroidered in white, the turn-up being blue with white embroidery and an embroidered grenade in the centre. Hair is natural, plaited and turned up under the cap. The coat was of red cloth cuffs, lapels and linings blue, the whole laced around in plain white lace. All loops pointed, eight on each lapel, three each side under the lapels, and one at the waist above the slit of the skirts, in the centre of the back, six each side on the slash pockets. The cuffs laced around the top with narrow lace, with broader lace underneath, the arrangement of the cuff slash on the sleeve is slightly different from that shown by Morier in 1751 (see sketches of cuffs detail). The skirts of the coat are not looped back, this was the normal position for Guard Order. The waistcoat of red cloth was edged and laced down the front in plain white. All buttons for coat and waistcoat in white metal with no design on the buttons. Breeches were of blue cloth, having four white metal buttons at the knee fastening, white stockings, Sandby shows the shoes as being white, this may be an oversight on the part of the artist, as the shoes were normally black. The equipment was a broad buff leather pouch-belt with a large brass buckle on the breast, and two above the pouch, brush and pickers on a small chain suspended from the end of the strap of the pouch-belt, used for cleaning burnt powder from the pan and vent of the musket. A brass match-case above the buckle on the breast (the 'badge' of the Grenadier) grenades by this time having fallen out of fashion. A large black polished pouch without any ornament. (Sandby or Morier do not show the Guards with the cartridges pouch worn in front round the waist like the Grenadiers of the Line Regiments.) The waist-belt, also of buff leather with brass buckle, suspended from this by a double frog, the Grenadier basket hilted sword, and bayonet, both having black leather scabbards with brass mounts.

This figure of a corporal shows detail as from Morier's paintings in the Royal Collection. The Grenadier cap is the same as described for the private but would now have the 'little flap' of red cloth instead of blue.

The coat similar except for the cuff detail (see sketch) and the corporal wears in addition a shoulder knot, denoting his rank on his right shoulder. The skirts in this case are buttoned back being for marching order.

The waistcoat and breeches are as described for the private, but here the corporal is wearing gaiters, white for full dress, brown sometimes black for service. In 1756 the Coldstream Guards ordered that their brown marching gaiters should be blackened and tops put on them. All buttons black. Black shoes.

Equipment was as for the private, but also a goat-skin knapsack and a grey canvas haversack, slung over each shoulder. A tin water-bottle on a cord would also be carried.

Field Day 1884, 1st Battalion Coldstream Guards. The Adjutant is shown in the Frock Uniform described in detail on page 60, talking to a company officer, while his Drummer/Bugler watches with interest. The Sergeant-Major keeps his eye on the ammunition supply, while a Field Officer in the background surveys the enemy position.

The men are wearing the 1882 Improved Valise Equipment described on page 62. It will be noticed that the bayonet scabbard hangs over the top of the haversack; this method is shown in many photographs.

The dress of all ranks in the picture is fully described in the text.

Coldstream Guards Orders of Dress 1894–1912. On the extreme left is a Sergeant in musketry order about 1910, he has the Short Magazine Lee Enfield Rifle and long bayonet. Second figure, is a Drill Sergeant in the red serge undress tunic with blue collar and round cuffs piped in narrow white lace, about 1896. The third figure is a Lance Sergeant about 1911, he wears the Atholl grey greatcoat with the rank badge on the lower right arm, the dress of Lance Sergeants is fully described on page 75. The fourth figure is a Band Master, about 1894. Guards Band Masters did not wear badges of rank on their arms.

The officer in the white Wolesley helmet belongs to the 3rd Battalion when stationed in Egypt from 1906 to 1911 and this is the full dress at that station.

The last figure is a Captain/adjutant of about 1912 wearing the blue forage cap and blue frock uniform, blue overalls and brass spurs, the dress is practically as it is today.

Fig 13: Grenadiers and Drummer, *c.* 1775

The detail of the illustration of the Grenadiers is based on some coloured drawings in the Grand Ducal Library at Darmstadt of Grenadiers of the three regiments of Foot Guards. The coats shown in the Darmstadt pictures are loose fitting and the skirts reach practically to the knees, the lapels are very long and reach well below the waist line.

The head-dress is of black bearskin, the fur running upwards and the front plate having a red background and the design of the Royal Arms being in white metal the red patch on the back of the cap possibly having the Royal Cypher within the Garter with the Crown above, embroidered in white in the centre, below at the back, a white metal grenade.

The coat of red cloth had a blue collar; lapels, cuffs and wings; the wings unfringed; all lace plain white, ten loops on each lapel set two by two; four on each cuff also set two by two; four on each pocket flap set two by two; and six on each wing set two by two. All buttons are white metal. Waistcoat white cloth with white metal buttons; breeches white and white canvas gaiters with white metal buttons. Black polished shoes. Equipment consisted of a whitened leather pouch-belt on which was worn the brass match-case, brass buckles at the rear above a black polished pouch, whitened leather waist-belt with a white metal buckle or clasp with the letters CG raised in the centre; the Grenadiers are not shown with swords, only the bayonet worn as illustrated, well to the front.

The detail for the drummer is taken from a WO 30/13A dated November 15 1773 from the Adjutant-General to the Secretary of the Clothing Board, which describes the alteration in the clothing of the Coldstream Guards.

The head-dress is the usual fur as described above; the coat has the same facings as the Grenadiers, but has extra lacing down the seams and six regular spaced laces, points down, on the outside of the sleeves. The wings are fringed; the body of the coat according to this order was laced 'State fashion' which would mean that drummers had a special type of lace, of what design it is difficult to say, the well-known 'fleur-de-lis' did not appear until much later. (An order of 1770 for the 1st Guards mentions the Drummers lace as having 'white silk and tinsel stripes in the lace', and an order of 1768 for the 3rd Guards states the drummers as having 'regimental lace'.) So it does appear that a special type of lace was indicated. The rest of the dress was as for the Grenadiers. The drum having a wooden shell painted blue, on which was painted the Royal Arms in full colour in the centre in front; the hoops red and the ties whitened.

Fig 14 : Sergeant, Private and Officer of the Guards Composite Battalion, *c.* 1777

On the outbreak of the war with the American Colonies, a Brigade Order of March 12 1776 stated 'His Majesty has been pleased to permit the officers of the detachments to make up a uniform with white lace, like the privates of their respective regiments, the sergeants to have their coats laced white instead of gold; the coats of all ranks of the Light Infantry to be cut according to the pattern issued for the occasion.'

The illustration shows this modified dress of the 2nd Guards detachment of the battalion companies. Head-dress is a black tricorne, white lace round the edge; black bow with white tie on the left side. (This head-dress for all ranks.) Hair is natural and tied in a queue. The coat for all ranks was of red cloth; the collar, lapels and cuffs of blue cloth; epaulettes with fringes on the right shoulders of both officer and sergeant, a plain shoulder strap on the left, and plain on both shoulders for the private. (The officers' epaulette and fringe in gold lace.) The shoulder straps were of red cloth edged with white lace. All buttons were of white metal. White cloth waistcoats and breeches, the buttons on these also of white metal. The sergeant has a crimson worsted sash, tied on the right, the officer one of crimson silk tied on the left. White woollen stockings with short black gaiters with white metal buttons. The equipment of whitened leather, black pouches, waist-belt having a regimental plate with the

(continued on page 33)

This sketch, of a typical morning drill parade, at the Guard's Depot, circa *1930, shows a Corporal instructing recruits in the turns of foot drill. The corporal is in service dress; the khaki tunic has two patch pockets with pleats on the breast and two ordinary pockets with flaps sewn into the lining on the hips. All these pockets were fastened with small brass regimental buttons, there were two more fastening the shoulder straps, whilst down the front of the tunic, were five larger brass regimental buttons. On the shoulder straps in brass was a Rose with CG. (The Guards did not in service dress wear collar badges.) White buff leather waist belt and frog for the bayonet was worn. The bayonet metal parts were burnished and the black scabbard which had a steel tip was highly polished. Khaki trousers were cut below the knee to give a smarter appearance when wearing puttees (this was quite contrary to orders). A spare pair of trousers of normal length were kept for wear on service, the puttees were worn over these and the trousers were 'box pleated'.*

Standing at ease watching the corporal are recruit Guardsmen. They are wearing the fatigue dress of brown canvas, with five small regimental buttons down the front of the jacket. The forage cap was worn in this order for drill.

Fig 15 : Officers of the Grenadier and Battalion Companies, *c.* 1789–1792

The head-dress for Officers of the Grenadier Company is a black bearskin now slightly altered in shape, the fur running downwards instead of up as before. The patch on the back in scarlet cloth, gold lace festoons and tassels, a gilt grenade in the centre of the back and a gilt Coat of Arms in the front. The hair was frizzed, powdered, plaited and turned up under the cap, tied with black ribbons. The coat shown is the 'Frock' or undress coat, it was of scarlet cloth with blue collar, lapels and cuffs, the epaulettes were also blue. The coat was edged round the collar, lapels and cuffs also epaulette straps with gold lace. (The epaulette straps on the first figure are of the older type as described above, but the officer shown from the rear wears epaulettes of the later type which are all of gold lace having a plain beading around the edge of the strap, gold crescents and bullion fringe; on the strap was the Garter Star in silver embroidery with a gold grenade above.) The pockets and skirts were also laced as shown in the illustration, the turnbacks were secured by a small piece of blue cloth with a sprig of foliage on each side in gold embroidery, over the centre of each a small gilt grenade. All buttons were gilt, the design featuring an eight-pointed star with the words 'Cm Gds' in the centre.

The gorget was of gilt metal with silver Royal Arms in the centre and on each side an engraved Garter Star, the whole tied with blue ribbon and rosettes. Equipment was of whitened leather having a small rectangular gilt belt-plate with the design of the Lion within a Crowned Garter (the late Mr P. W. Reynolds records that all the Grenadier companies of the Regiments of Foot Guards had this plate). The cartouche box or pouch, black polished leather, the badge a gilt Garter Star with a grenade in gilt above. The officers had a short bayonet for their fusils, this having a black leather scabbard with a gilt tip. (On May 8 1792, a General Order, ordering all officers of Grenadier companies to make use of their swords, instead of fusils and bayonets and to give up these along with the pouch-belt and pouch. The sword to be their only weapon.) A white waist-coat and breeches with gilt buttons, crimson sash, and soft boots with turnover tops in black leather, completed their dress.

The head-dress for the Officer of the Battalion Company was a black felt bicorne with gold cord tie and black silk bow. Hair was frizzed and powdered tied in a club with black silk bow and ribbons.

This officer wears the full dress coat which differs from the 'Frock' described above in having a scarlet collar and the buttonholes laced with gold loops and an extra ring of gold lace round the cuffs; the pockets were laced similar to the frock but in much broader gold lace, there was no lace running down the seam from the waist to the bottom of the skirt. The lace edging the turnbacks had a fine blue feathering on the outside edge. The turnback fastening was the same as the Grenadiers but had no grenade. Buttons were gilt as described above. The epaulette for battalion companies was worn on the right shoulder only, for junior officers, and in this case of the same design as described for the Grenadier officer but omitting the grenade.

The gorget was the same as the Grenadiers. The sword belt of whitened leather; gilt shoulder-belt plate with beaded edge, silver Garter Star with blue enamel Garter and red cross gilt motto. Sword had a gilt hilt, gold and crimson sword knot, the blade decorated with a blue and gilt filligree design. The remainder of the dress was as for the Grenadiers.

Fig 16: Corporal and Private of the Battalion Company in Marching Order, 1790

The figures are based on the water-colours of E. Dayes and a series of plates illustrating the Manual Exercise with the musket and bayonet which was published in 1790.

The head-dress is the black cocked hat, plain without lace and having stiffeners back and front, a worsted loop and regimental button with a white feather plume with a black tip. The hat had a black tape sewn each side, which was tied together under the hair at the back to keep the hat in place on the head. Hair was clubbed and tied with black ribbon, larded and floured. The shirt frill and sleeve ends were white. The coat was red with blue collar, lapels, cuffs and epaulettes straps, the whole laced around with plain white lace, loops set two by two on lapels, cuffs and pocket flaps. All buttons were white metal.

The corporal wears a white silk fringed epaulette on his right shoulder and a plain one on the left; the private, of course, has two plain worsted epaulettes. Waistcoats and breeches are in white cloth with black gaiters, all having white metal buttons. Shoes are black.

Equipment is whitened leather, the pouch-belt having brass buckles and tips, and black polished pouch with brass Garter Star badge. Black canvas knapsack had the Garter Star painted in the centre in full colour, white star, blue garter, red cross and lettered in gold on the garter: 'COLDSTREAM GUARDS'. Support straps were all whitened leather. Bayonet scabbard was black with brass mounts. Whitened leather sling and brass runner buckle were supplied for the musket.

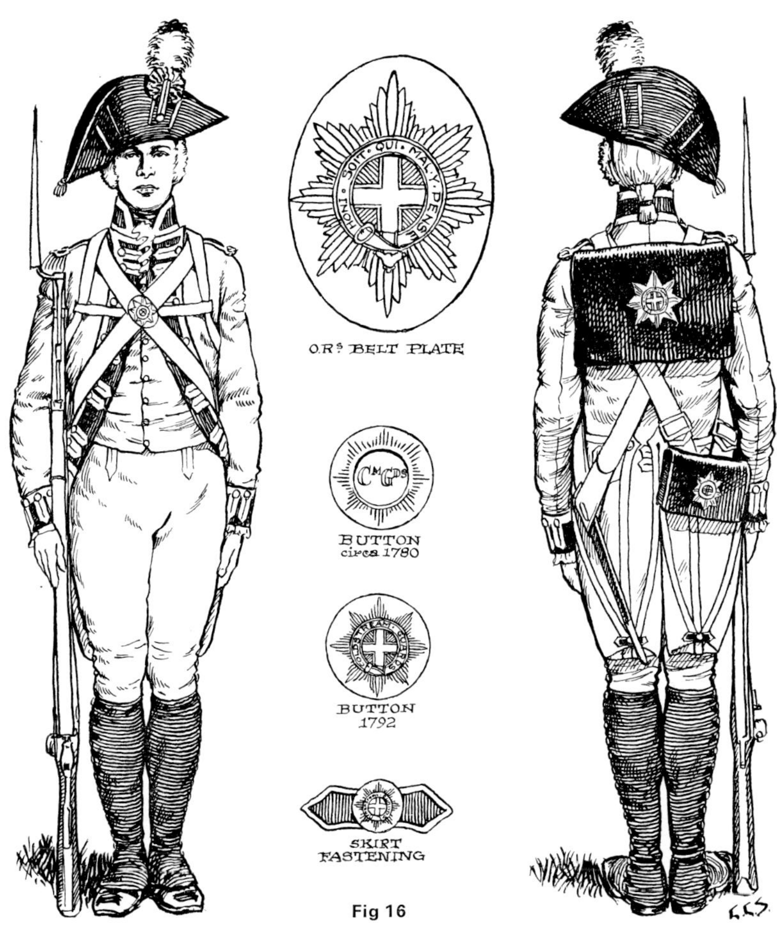

Button c. 1780: *A pewter button of the other ranks, the button was flat with the design in low relief. Officers had a similar design, but in gilt metal.*

Button 1792: *Other ranks button in pewter, the design was also in low relief and flat.*

The officer's button of this period was flat gilt and the same design but engraved.

Belt-Plate ORs: *This plate was brass and had the design die-stamped.*

Fig 17 : Sergeants of the Battalion and Grenadier Companies, c. 1790

The uniform detail of these two figures is from contemporary water-colour by E. Dayes and show clearly the dress of sergeants of the 2nd or Coldstream Guards at this period.

The battalion company sergeant in Full Dress has the black felt cocked hat with stiffeners in the front and back, no lace round the brim. (In 1790 it was ordered that the hats of the NCOs and men of the Foot Guards to be without

lace.) A gold lace hoop and feather white with a black tip. Hair frizzed, powdered, clubbed and tied with a black ribbon. Shirt frill white. The coat was of scarlet cloth with blue collar; lapels epaulette straps and cuffs, all edged around in gold lace, gold lace buttonhole loops set two by two on cuffs, lapels and pocket flaps. All buttons brass, the design being an eight-pointed star with the words 'Cm Gds' in the centre. The epaulette on the right shoulder is fringed but on the left plain.

White cloth waistcoat with small brass buttons of the same design as the coat; crimson worsted sash; white cloth breeches and black gaiters both having brass buttons. Sword-belt whitened leather; sword brass hilt and gold sword knot; black leather scabbard with brass mountings.

The Sergeant of the Grenadier Company in Full Dress wears a black bearskin with gold festoon and tassels, white feather plume; brass Royal Arms plate in front, scarlet patch on back of cap and a brass grenade underneath. Hair is frizzed, plaited and turned up under the cap, tied with black ribbons. Shirt frill white. Coat the same as for the battalion company sergeant, except for blue cloth wings laced in gold and fringed. Fringed epaulettes over the top on both shoulders. The turnbacks fastened by brass grenades. The rest of the uniform follows the battalion sergeant's dress. Equipment consists of cross belts in whitened leather, black polished pouch, the buckles on the pouch-belt brass, brass Garter Star badge on the pouch with brass grenade above. Short bayonet in black scabbard with brass tip, fusil having white leather sling. Belt-plate for the Battalion Sergeant is brass having the Garter Star engraved. The same for the Grenadier but in addition it had a small grenade above. Canes for both are wood with brass top and ferrule.

Fig 18 : Musicians in Full Dress, 1792

Very little is known of the dress of the Musicians of the Army at this time, and it is only from regimental orders and clothing bills that it is possible to get any idea of what their appearance would have been. There is also in existence a very few paintings and prints showing bandsmen, usually as part of a parade and consequently very indistinct in detail, but there are one or two that do give very good detail and with these and the several references to their dress in orders, etc, we are able to construct a fair representation of the dress.

In the case of the Guards we are fortunate in having a print of this period showing the relief of the Guard at St James's Palace, though no regiment is specified, it at least, gives us the general appearance of the Guards' musicians. (My own impression is that this print is of the band of the 1st Guards.) There is also a mezzotint of a negro Tambourinist of the 2nd Guards which gives the detail of the 2nd Guards lace arrangement. (See Fig 19.)

From these two prints I have endeavoured to reconstruct the dress of the bandsmen of the 2nd or Coldstream Guards. The head-dress is the black felt bicorne with the usual stiffeners, a black ribbon cockade with a silver lace tie. The edge of the hat lined with red feathers, and a red over white feather plume. Hair is powdered and clubbed. The coat is of scarlet cloth, with blue collar, epaulette straps and wings, also blue cuffs, all laced around with silver lace, silver lace down the front of each edge of the coat and round the turnbacks. Buttonhole lace loops were silver with a feathered cloth blue edge. Pocket flaps were edged with silver lace and had two pairs of loops on each. The back of the coat would probably be laced down the seams. At the waist, by the side of each pocket was a button, and between these, two silver loops above the skirt slit. All buttons were white metal. Waistcoat and breeches were white cloth, with white metal buttons. As the bandsmen are in full dress they are wearing the long white gaiters with black leather garters under the knee. The sword-belt would have been of whitened leather, having the usual brass belt-plate with the Garter Star embossed as for the other ranks. The sword had a brass hilt, black scabbard and brass tip.

The musicians are playing a Serpent, an early brass instrument, and an early example of a clarinet.

The 2nd Guards appear to have adopted silver lace for their bandsmen, possibly to make a marked difference between them and the bandsmen of the 1st Guards, who wore gold.

Fig 18

Fig 19: John Fraser, Tambourine Player, *c.* 1790

This is a reproduction of a coloured mezzotint of a negro bandsman by the name of John Fraser. His dress consists of a white turban with a silver crescent and blue beads, these possibly at the back of the turban as well. From the top of the turban (not very clear in the repro- duction) is a red feather plume with a blue top. The jacket, has what appears to be short sleeves with silver and blue fringes, and is of scarlet cloth with silver lace on blue backing, the bastion style loops have tasselled ends. The wings are sewn down on the shoulders, and are of blue cloth edged in silver lace, the shoulder straps are also of blue cloth. The lower part of the sleeve is of white cloth and laced on the seams in silver lace with blue backing, these could be the sleeves of the waistcoat. He wears a silver collar and bracelets, all engraved with the Garter Star. He wears a blue sash with silver edging. A white leather sword-belt featured a belt-plate with Garter Star engraved.

The tambourine hoops are red on the outside and blue inside, edged with gold, all decorations gold.

Fig 20: Privates of the Light Company, 1794

It was not until 1793, on April 15 of that year to be precise, owing no doubt to the troubles in Europe, that the Guards were ordered to form again Light Infantry Companies, but this time by this order we find there was to be one for each battalion of Foot Guards; four for the 1st Guards, while the 2nd (Coldstream) and 3rd (Scots) were to have two each.

The illustration shows the dress of these companies of the 2nd Guards. The details of the uniform have been taken from a contemporary water colour by Dayes and a print by Scott of the Coldstream Guards. The head-dress is a black round hat with a fur crest and a large green hackle feather, the rim is held by black ties. The hair is natural colour and plaited, turned up under the hat and tied with black ribbons. The coatee is faced blue, having a blue collar, cuffs, lapels and shoulder straps, these last are laced all round and fringed with white worsted. All lace and loops plain white worsted; three sets of loops in twos on each lapel and two sets on each cuff. The pocket flaps on the skirts, set diagonally and laced around also, had two sets of loops in twos; the lapels and cuffs were laced along the edge with plain white. All buttons in white metal had the design of the Garter Star; on the garter instead of the usual motto, were the words 'Coldstream Guards'. (This design was adopted by the Regiment in 1792.)

A white waistcoat with white metal buttons, white pantaloons and black shoes were worn. The equipment was of whitened leather, having brass buckles on the pouch-belt. The pouch in black polished leather had the badge

of the Garter Star in brass in the centre. The shoulder-belt plate of brass, was die struck, the design being the Garter Star (at this time the flank companies appeared to have no distinction in these belt-plates, ie, a bugle horn or grenade). The bayonet scabbard was of black leather with brass tip and pin for the frog.

Fig 21 : Officers of the Light Company, *c.* 1800

The detail for this illustration is taken from a water-colour sketch, by Robert Dighton, junior, of about 1800. The head-dress shown was introduced in 1800, commonly called the 'Stove Pipe' shako (the name Shako is derived from the Hungarian word meaning a military cylindrical cap with a peak), at first this shako was lacquered and had a back peak, able to be turned down in foul weather, but in 1806 a similar pattern, but made in felt, without the back peak was introduced. Normally officers of the Infantry wore the cocked hat, but officers of the Light Companies of infantry regiments, the Light Infantry and Rifle Regiments wore the shako, only wearing the cocked hat on special occasions. For officers the bugle horn sign was worn in front in gilt metal, a black silk Hanoverian cockade with a regimental button and long green feather plume above. The hair was powdered and turned up in a plait and tied with black ribbons.

The coatee was the 'frock' with a plain blue collar, lapels and cuffs edged in gold lace. The wings had scarlet shells edged with gold lace and fringed, the strap was gold lace with a silver embroidered Garter Star with a silver embroidered bugle horn above. All buttons were gilt having the design of the Garter Star but having the garter inscribed 'Coldstream Guards'. The buttons were set two by two and were of a smaller type than those worn by the Grenadier and Battalion companies. Another difference was that the Light Companies' coatee had the pocket flaps on the back skirts set on the slant instead of horizontal as was the case with the rest of the regiment. The gorget was gilt bearing the Royal Arms in silver with the Garter Star engraved on each side. The shoulder-belt plate was oval, gilt with a beaded rim, the Garter Star

silver and the garter gilt, with the motto in pierced letters on a blue enamel ground; the cross was in red enamel, a bugle horn being above the star.

The sword-belt was white leather and the curved Light Infantry sword was carried in a frog (later the Light Infantry adopted slings). The sword hilt was gilt with a gold and crimson sword knot, the blade had a blue and gold filligree design extending down half its length. The scabbard was black leather with gilt mounts. A crimson silk sash of normal pattern was worn, but later having for the Light Infantry cords and tassels. White kerseymere breeches and black boots with turnover tops completed the uniform.

Fig 22: Private Battalion Company, Marching Order, Corporal Light Company, Review Order, Private Grenadier Company, Guard Order, *c.* 1803

The Private of the Battalion Company has the Black 'Stove Pipe' shako, the large brass shako-plate bearing the universal Crown and Trophies of flags, trumpets, etc, with the Crowned Lion beneath, but in the centre, in place of the usual Royal Cypher the regimental badge of the Star of the Garter. The plume is a white over red tuft. Hair would be tied in a queue. The coatee of brick red cloth had a blue collar, epaulette straps and cuffs, the lace being plain white. The loops down the front of the coatee were set two by two, the same on the cuffs and back pockets flaps (these last for battalion and grenadier companies being set horizontally). The lace ran round the top and bottom of the collar, epaulette straps, down the front edge of the coatee and round the skirts. The epaulettes for battalion companies had tufted ends. The buttons were all of white metal. This coatee was the earlier type being larger and roomier than the later type soon to appear; the waistcoat could still be seen in the front.

Equipment was of whitened leather with a black ammunition pouch having a brass Garter Star badge. The bayonet scabbard was black leather with a brass tip and pin for the frog. The canvas knapsack was painted black and had the

Garter Star painted on, but on the garter the words 'COLDSTREAM GUARDS'. Grey greatcoat rolled on top (Greatcoats became a general issue in 1801, and was to last each man three years, the cost being 14s 6d each. Before this each regiment had on charge only a certain number of 'Watch Coats' for sentry duty.) The breeches were of white kerseymere with black gaiters having white metal buttons and black shoes. (On service ticken or canvas overalls were issued, sometimes buttoned all the way up the outside seams or just at the ankle, these last usually referred to as 'Russian Duck' overalls.)

The Corporal of the Light Company is very similar to the above description except for the following points: The shako-plate would be the same in all details but would possibly have a bugle horn in place of the Crowned Lion at the bottom, and a green tuft plume. His hair, plaited and turned up under the shako, was tied with black ribbons. The coatee had blue wings, fringed and laced in white, having three sets of loops set in twos. The rank badges, at this time on the right arm only, in plain regimental lace for all companies. The pockets on the skirts set diagonally and all buttons were of a slightly smaller size.

It will be noted that the Guards had two brass buckles at the pouch end of the pouch-belt; this was peculiar to Guards Regiments only, and all companies had these.

The Grenadier again was similar to the above description of the Battalion Company Private except for the following differences: head-dress a black bearskin with white festoons and tassels; white feather plume; white metal Royal Arms badge, wings on the coatee as for the Light Company. He still wears the relic of the old Grenadier match-case on the pouch-belt and being in Guard Order has the greatcoat slung over his right shoulder by a brown leather strap with a brass buckle.

The shoulder-belt plate for all three was of brass with a stamped out design of the Garter Star, but the Light Company had a small bugle horn engraved over the top and the Grenadier a small grenade.

The shako was also worn by the Grenadier Companies on the occasions when the bearskin cap was not worn; the shako had a white worsted tuft plume, and on the Hanoverian cockade (in the case of the other ranks this was made in tooled leather blackened, the officers being made in silk) a small brass grenade was worn instead of a Regimental button as worn by the Light and Battalion companies. The shako-plate was exactly the same as for the battalion companies.

Fig 23: Sergeant, Drill Order, Private, Guard Order, Battalion Company, c. 1814

The Sergeant wears a black felt shako (this shako replaced the old Stove Pipe about 1812, and was known as the 'Belgic' or 'Waterloo' shako), with gold festoons and tassels: patent leather peak, brass shako-plate, black leather cockade on the left fastened with a brass regimental button, and a feather plume, white over red. Scarlet coatee had blue collar, epaulette straps and cuffs, all lace gold. Buttons were brass. Gold lace chevrons had blue cloth backing on the right arm only (the Grenadier and Light companies' NCOs having their chevrons on both arms). White leather sword-belt with brass belt-plate and a sword with a brass hilt of regimental design, black leather scabbard with brass mounts were regulation wear. Sash was crimson.

White cloth breeches, black linen gaiters with brass buttons a cane brass tip, gold cord and tassel completed the uniform.

The Private has a black felt shako as for the sergeant, but with white worsted festoons and tassels. Plume was a worsted tuft, white over red. Coatee is of red cloth with all lace plain white, the lace arrangement as for the

Fig 24 : Officers, Battalion Company, Frock Uniform and Full Dress, 1815

The officer in Frock Uniform wears a head-dress of black felt with a gilt vandyked edge (this edging was taken into wear for only a short time. Possibly intended to stiffen the felt 'false front' of the cap, it seems to have been also worn by bandsmen. A plain brass strip was also worn as well by the other ranks, instead of the vandyked pattern. It was replaced by $\frac{3}{8}$ inch black braid. Gold and crimson festoons and tassels and a black silk cockade on the left, were secured by a gilt regimental button. Feather plume was white over red. The shako-plate gilt featured a silver Garter Star having a blue enamel Garter and red cross. Black patent leather drooping peak was fitted on the shako.

Coatee was of scarlet cloth with blue collar, cuffs, lapels; all lace gold. The lace ran round top and bottom of the blue collar, round the edges of the lapels and edge of the turnbacks. The pocket flaps were also edged with gold lace and two strips ran from the waist buttons down to the bottom of the skirts at the back. Between the buttons at the back was a diamond of gold lace. The cuffs had gold lace round the top. All buttons were gilt.

The epaulettes were of gold lace, corded round the edge with alternate blue and gold twist. The crescent was of gold bullion edged with blue and gold cord twist and with bullion fringes. As this officer's rank is a captain, he wears two epaulettes and has a crown above the half crescent on each strap. Also shown in wear is the crimson sash, whitened buffalo leather sword belt, belt plate in gilt with a silver Garter Star, blue enamel Garter and red cross. The plate had a beaded rim. Straight sword had a gilt hilt with ivory grip, and gold and crimson sword knot. White breeches and black Hessian boots with black tassels completed this dress.

The Officer in Full Dress wears a black bicorn edged with gold lace, gold tie and button, and black silk cockade. He has a white over red feather plume and gold cord round the crown of the hat, only the gold tassel from this showing.

The coat is of scarlet cloth with scarlet collar, blue cuffs. All lace gold; turnbacks white cloth, on these the gold lace is 'feathered' on the inside edge (ie, next to the white cloth of the turnback) in blue cloth. Turnback fastening is of blue cloth with gold embroidered foliage spray.

White breeches and long white gaiters with black buttons, crimson sash, white buffalo leather sword-belt, and all appointments are as described for officer in Frock Uniform.

The front of the Full Dress coat had blue lapels heavily laced in gold, ten loops in pairs with gilt buttons, the edges of the lapels laced around in gold. Epaulettes are the same as described for Frock uniform.

Fig 25 : Officer and Sergeant of the Light Company, 1815

The Officer wears a black felt shako, with the 'false front' bound in black braid, gold and crimson festoons and tassels, gilt shako-plate with silver Garter Star with blue enamel Garter and red cross in the centre, gilt bugle horn badge over the top of the shako-plate. He also wears a black silk cockade with the regimental button in the centre, from which protrudes a green feather plume.

The coatee is of scarlet cloth, with blue collar and cuffs (this is the frock coatee), all gold lace similar to the description for the battalion company officer, except that buttons were smaller in size. The skirt ornaments were silver embroidered bugle horns on blue cloth backing. Gold lace epaulette straps were edged with gold and blue cord twist. The wings were a scarlet cloth shell, edged with gold lace and having a gold fringe. A Garter Star in silver embroidery was on the strap with silver embroidered bugle horn above. At the throat was worn a black neckerchief with a white shirt frill.

The sword-belt and slings were of whitened leather, with gilt buckles. The belt-plate was of gilt with the usual Garter Star in silver and blue and red enamel, but in the case of the Light Company a small silver bugle horn above the star. A silver whistle and a chain was worn with a spy glass carried in a brown leather case and strap. White gloves were worn and the sash was crimson with crimson cords and tassels. The trousers were grey overall with leather 'cuffs'. Black half boots were worn underneath.

The sword was a small curved sabre, with a gilt hilt, a lion's head pommel and black and silver wire grip. The blade halfway down was blue with gilt filligree design. Gold and crimson sword knot was carried on the sword.

The Sergeant wears a black felt shako similar to the officer, with gold lace festoons and tassels, brass shako-plate and bugle horn and a black leather cockade with regimental button and green feather plume.

The coatee was of scarlet cloth with a blue collar, epaulette straps, wing shells and cuffs. All lace was gold with brass buttons. Chevrons on both arms were in gold lace with blue cloth backing. Turnbacks were in white cloth.

Equipment worn was of whitened leather belts with a brass belt-plate embossed with Garter Star and bugle horn above, silver whistle and chain. Canvas haversack; blue-grey painted water-bottle with 'Cd Gds. L.J.' in white lettering. Brass hilted sword, black knapsack with Garter Star painted in the centre, grey overcoat roll strapped on top and black ammunition pouch (smaller than the men's) with Garter Star and bugle horn in brass, completed the equipment.

Grey overall trousers were worn with small grey (or black) gaiters. (In some prints and pictures the Guards are shown with their overall trousers tucked inside black half gaiters.) The sash was crimson.

Fig 26: Drum Major and Bugler in Service Dress, *c.* 1815

The detail for this illustration is from Finart's contemporary drawings and drawings by Cramer of the Foot Guards.

The Drum Major wears a black felt shako, the edge of the false 'front' bound in white metal of a vandyked pattern. The festoons were probably of silver with silver tassels. The Shako-plate was of a special design of a Crown surmounting a trophy of flags, in the centre a Garter Star. The whole appears to be embossed in brass. Black cockade had a silver button in the centre; from this was worn a white feather plume.

The coatee was of scarlet cloth, with a blue collar, lapels and cuffs. The epaulette straps were also of blue cloth edged in, possibly, silver lace. Silver lace loops on the lapels were set in pairs, the edge of the lapels laced, as well as the seams of the coatee. Six inverted chevrons of lace were worn on the sleeves, the cuffs edged around and four loops on each cuff. All buttons were silver.

The drum sash was of blue cloth, edged in silver lace having a silver fringe at the end, Gold embroidered Crown with crimson cap, black drumsticks with

silver mounts and the Royal Cypher in gold embroidery underneath. Crimson sash round the waist had large tassels on the right. The sword-belt was of whitened leather with brass belt-plate and sword hilt in a black scabbard with brass mounts. The breeches were white with black linen gaiters with white metal buttons.

The drum major's staff was black with silver top and crown, silver cord and tassels, and tip.

The Bugler wears a head-dress similar to the drum major's but the festoons and tassels were of white worsted. The plume was a worsted tuft, white with a red top.

The coatee is of scarlet cloth, with a blue collar, epaulette straps and cuffs. Collar was laced around with plain white lace as also the cuffs and epaulette straps, four lace loops on each cuff. The lace on the breast was narrow, plain white with tasselled ends. All buttons white metal. White leather sword-belt, brass belt-plate, short brass hilted drummer's sword, black scabbard, and brass mounts completed this dress.

The bugle is of silver with yellow cords and tassels. The breeches and gaiters are as for the drum major.

One would have expected the lace on the buglers' coatee to have been of Drummers lace with blue fleur-de-lis, which makes one suspect that the lace of this particular figure is of silver, especially as the lace on the front of the coatee is very similar to that of the negro bandsmen who all had silver lace in the Coldstream Guards.

Fig 27 : Officer and Sergeant of the Grenadier Company, 1816

The dress details for this illustration are from several contemporary sources such as Sauerweid, Charles Hamilton-Smith, and Hawkes and Co pattern books.

The Officer, based mainly on drawings by Sauerweid, wears the Grenadier cap of a black bearskin, with gold and crimson festoons and tassels, gilt grenade above gilt Royal Arms, white feather plume on the left and possibly gilt chin scales, fastened up at the back, of the cap. (It does seem from evidence that these chin scales were worn. There is a contemporary print in the Guards'

Museum at Wellington Barracks, of Sgt Skinner of the 1st Guards wearing a Grenadier cap of similar design that has chin scales.)

The coatee is the frock as described before, very similar to the Light Company officer, but having larger buttons, the same as for the battalion companies, of regimental design, also having gold embroidered grenades above the Garter Star on epaulette straps, instead of a bugle horn. The gorget gilt with silver Royal Arms. This officer wears his Waterloo medal.

He wears a crimson sash with a sword-belt and belt-plate as described for the battalion company officer in Fig 24. (The grenade that was originally placed above the Star for the Grenadier company, seems to have disappeared after about 1805 from the belt-plate.) The sword was the same pattern as the battalion officer (officers of the Grenadier company did adopt the curved sabre at times).

White breeches and black Hessian boots with black tassels completed this dress.

The Sergeant wears the Grenadier cap with gold festoons and tassels and a gilt grenade at the back. It is possible that chin scales were worn. Brass plate featured the Royal Arms.

The coatee of scarlet cloth is as described for the Light Company sergeant in all details, except that the buttons were of normal size. (When the coatee was first adopted the Grenadier and Battalion Companies had their pocket flaps set on horizontally, while the Light had theirs sloping diagonally. By about 1812 all companies favoured the pockets being set as the Light Company.)

The sword was of regimental design having the Garter Star badge set in the brass knuckle guard, with a gold sword knot. Scabbard was black with gilt mounts. Belt-plate all brass as for sergeant of battalion in Fig 23. White breeches and long white gaiters, with black buttons are shown, the figure being in Full Dress.

Fig 27

Fig 28: Officers, Battalion and Grenadier Companies, *c.* 1821

The dress detail is from contemporary water-colours and sketches of the Coldstream Guards by Denis Dighton.

The Officer of a Battalion Company in Full Dress, wears a head-dress of a black felt shako with gold lace round the top, black crêpe or silk Hanoverian cockade, gold festoons and acorns, silver Garter Star with blue enamelled Garter and red cross, and a black patent leather drooping peak. Side ornaments holding the gilt chin scales, were the Tudor Rose. Plume was white over red feather.

The coatee was of scarlet cloth with scarlet collar, blue lapels and cuffs. The lapels were laced in gold, in pairs, the cuffs laced around the top with narrow lace, and round the middle in broad lace. Pockets were laced all round as was the edge of the turnbacks, all in fact, similar to the Full Dress coat as described in Fig 24. A crimson sash was worn with a sword-belt of white buffalo leather. The belt-plate was gilt with a beaded edge, Silver Garter Star with blue enamelled Garter and red cross.

A straight sword was carried similar to the type described for the officers of the Battalion Company in Fig 24. The gorget was gilt with silver Royal Arms, blue ribbon and rosettes. Epaulettes were gold lace strap edged with gold cord, bullion full crescent and fringe. As this figure is a captain, he has a gold embroidered Crown within each crescent.

The breeches and long gaiters were white with black buttons.

The Officer of the Grenadier Company in Frock Uniform, wears a black bearskin cap with gold and crimson festoons and tassels, a gilt plate with the Royal Arms embossed and a white feather plume on the left.

The coatee was of scarlet cloth with a blue collar, lapels, epaulette straps and wing shells, also the cuffs. The collar, lapels, epaulettes and wings, turnbacks, pockets, skirt seams and cuffs were all edged in gold lace. The skirt ornaments were of blue cloth with a spray of foliage embroidered in gold, on top of this a gold grenade. A crimson sash with white buffalo leather sword-belt and the belt-plate was worn as described above. The sword was a sabre with gilt hilt, lion head pommel and a gold and crimson sword knot. Blue-black undress trousers are worn here.

Fig 29 : Sergeants of the Light Company, 1819–1822

The dress details for these figures are taken from contemporary drawings and water-colours by Denis Dighton, and a painting of the Guard Changing at St James's Palace, 1820.

The Sergeant in Full Dress of 1822 wears the felt Regency shako first introduced in 1816, but modified in 1822 by having the lace removed from round the top and the turned up peak at the back removed. The brass chin scales are tied up in this case, over the top of the tooled leather cockade, on which was a brass bugle horn. The feather plume was 9 inches long and coloured deep green. The brass shako-plate is the usual Garter Star

The coatee was of scarlet cloth with blue collar, epaulette straps, wings and cuffs. All lace is gold with gold chevrons on blue backing on each arm. The crimson sash was tied at the rear. Note the cuff slash of scarlet cloth, edged white with four gold loops in pairs; this alteration to the cuffs was authorized a year or two previously.

Equipment was of whitened leather with a brass belt-plate (Dighton shows no bugle horn above the star on this). Black pouch-belt with a brass Garter Star and the sword and bayonet in a double frog.

Breeches and long gaiters were white with black buttons.

The Sergeant in Drill Order of 1819 wears the shako as it was before the modification referred to above, ie, the shako is of black felt with a band of gold lace round the top and has a black turned up peak behind. The brass chin scales are tied up over the tooled leather cockade with brass bugle horn. The plume is a green feather above the brass Garter Star shako-plate.

The coatee similar in all respects to the above description (except for the cuffs which had not altered from the 1815 coatee) has turnbacks of white cloth with brass bugle horn ornaments.

The sword had a brass hilt and gold sword knot, the scabbards of the bayonet and sword were black leather with brass mounts. The pouch was black with the Garter Star badge in brass below a crimson sash tied at the rear.

White breeches and black gaiters were worn with brass buttons.

Fig 30: Private of the Grenadier Company in Drill Order, *c*. 1822

Fig 30 is a series of photographs showing four views of a wood carving by the author, one of a series of figures of English Regiments that he is at present working on. The figure is 25½ inches in height overall, and has been carved from a solid block of Limewood with no parts made separately, the whole, including base being of one piece. It gives a good idea of dress at this particular period. The dress detail is partly from Denis Dighton's sketches and an old Drill Manual, His Majesty's Regulations 1828, by Major T. L. Mitchell published in 1828. (The figures depicted are of the Coldstream Guards.)

The Private of the Grenadier Company in Drill Order wears a shako the same as described for the sergeant of the Light Company, 1822, in Fig 29, except that the plume in this case is all white. (The Grenadier company in full dress wore the bearskin cap, but on occasions wore the shako instead).

The coatee was of red cloth with a blue collar, epaulette straps wing shells and cuffs, all lace being plain white. The collar was laced around the top and bottom and had a loop of lace on each side of the front. Epaulette and wing shells were laced with a worsted fringe along the edge of the shell. Eight lace loops in pairs were worn on the breast. The cuff slash of red cloth was piped in white with four lace loops on each. The pocket flaps were piped the same, also with four loops on each, in pairs. The turnbacks were white with brass grenade skirt ornament.

Equipment was of whitened leather with a brass belt-plate, brass buckles on the pouch-belt and a black polished pouch with brass Garter Star badge. All buttons were of white metal. The trousers or overalls were white, these being summer wear. On the figure the black gaiters can be seen over the shoes.

Fig 31 : Officers in Winter Dress and Full Dress, Summer, *c.* 1832

Dress details for these figures are from a contemporary print from the Spooner Upright series by Mansion and Exchauzier and the paintings of Dubois Drahonet.

The head-dress of the bearskin cap was now worn by the whole of the Coldstream Regiment of Foot Guards as mentioned in the introduction to this book. The Coldstream had adopted the red plume on the right side of the cap, under which two large gold tassels hung. In the front was the badge of the Rose with the Crown above, while at the back, more towards the top was the Garter Star in silver with blue enamelled Garter and red cross.

The coatee was of scarlet cloth, with blue patches on each side of the front of the collar, leaving it scarlet at the back. This coatee was quite plain with two rows of buttons narrowing towards the bottom with the buttons being set on in pairs and having vertical pockets and flap on the cuffs. All lace was gold of similar type and design as that used in Full Dress today. This covered practically the whole of the blue patches on the collar. In the centre, on each side, was a silver embroidered Garter Star. Four gold lace loops were worn on each cuff slash and pocket flap, set on in pairs. All buttons were gilt, the design on these similar to the type described in Fig 21 except that now the motto 'Honi Soit Qui Mal Y Pense' replaced the words 'Coldstream Guards' on the Garter, the design was in relief and the button convex. The turnbacks were of white cloth having silver embroidered Garter Stars as skirt ornaments. Large gold lace epaulettes were worn with gilt crescents, and an embroidered Tudor Rose within the crescent on the strap, and as the rank of these two officers is captain, an embroidered Crown above the rose.

The sword-belt was of whitened leather, the belt-plate, now square in shape, of gilt with a matted surface, the Garter Star in the same form as described for the oval plate. The sword was now of a different design with a gilt hilt, and gold and crimson sword knot. The scabbard was black polished leather with a gilt tip. A crimson sash (in Full Dress a gold sash with crimson stripes and gold tassels was worn). Dark blue-grey trousers with a broad scarlet stripe were worn in the winter months; white trousers in the summer. Dark blue trousers with a gold stripe were authorized for Full Dress.

The officer on the left is in winter dress with blue-grey trousers with scarlet stripes, and a crimson sash.

The officer on the right is in Full Dress in the summer, with white trousers and the full dress sash.

Fig 32 : Drummers, *c.* 1845

In an article in volume 20 of the Journal of the Society of Army Historical Research *by the Reverend Percy Sumner, he gave a very good description of a drummer's coat of the Coldstream Guards which was taken from an actual coat in the possession of the regiment. From this and other references, notably another article in the same Journal, Vol 33 by W. Y. Carman describing a drummer's dress of the Coldstream Guards circa 1851, I have constructed this line drawing of the drummers.*

The head-dress was a black bearskin, with the red horse hair plume and brass chin chain. The coat was of scarlet cloth, having blue collar and cuffs. All lace was of the Royal pattern, white with blue fleur-de-lis. The Coldstream was distinctive in having blue and white fringed epaulettes (both the other Guards Regiments having wings). Another distinction was the drum carriage, laced in Royal lace, this was still in existence after the Crimean War, as it is shown in an illustration featured in the Illustrated London News *of April 26, 1856 describing the then new double-breasted tunic that had just been issued to the Coldstream.*

The collar of the coatee had a blue and white fringe, and at the back, between the buttons at the waist was also a fringe of blue and white; all buttons pewter. White embroidered stars on blue cloth were worn with a small button in the centre as a skirt ornament. The cuff slashes were of scarlet cloth, on which were four loops and buttons set two by two.

Equipment was of whitened leather, the pouch being whitened also (earlier this had been black). The belt-plate was of brass having the Garter Star embossed. The drummer's sword had a brass hilt.

The drum had a brass shell, the front painted blue, having the Royal Arms and trophies of flags in full heraldic colours also painted thereon. The drum hoops were coloured in the distinctive Coldstream way, ie, having a blue worm on a white ground and red edges. (The other Regiments of Foot Guards had a white worm on a blue ground with red edges.) The drum ties were white, the drumsticks black.

Fig 33: Corporal and Privates of the 1st Battalion, *c.* 1850–1855

This illustration gives the dress of the other ranks as it was when the regiment went to the Crimea. The bearskin cap was worn at first but soon discarded for the more comfortable forage cap. The men in this illustration are armed with the 1842 pattern percussion musket, but later the regiment received an issue of the new Minie rifle.

The bearskin cap shape can be clearly seen in the drawing, as there is a side, front and three-quarter rear view. The red plume is on the right side and the chin scales are brass.

The coatee for all three figures was of red cloth with blue collar and cuffs. The cuffs had a small slash flap in red cloth, on which were four lace loops set in pairs in plain white. Epaulettes are white and fringed; the collar ornamented with white embroidered Garter Stars. The coat tails have white turnbacks, on which were Garter Star ornaments on blue cloth patches. The buttons were of an alloy containing copper, which gave them a slightly brassy look. The corporal's stripes plain white tape.

The trousers were the white summer issue; in winter dark Oxford mixture trousers with a red stripe about a quarter of an inch wide down the outside seams, would be worn.

Equipment was of whitened leather, the pouch and bayonet belts being worn over the shoulders (the Guards wore this equipment in the Crimea). The black pouch had the brass Garter Star badge on the flap, the pouch-belt having the two brass buckles and tips above the pouch. The bayonet scabbard was black with brass mounts. The knapsack was black with the Garter Star badge in the centre. The mess tin covered in black oilskin was secured next to the grey greatcoat roll.

The belt-plate was square with rounded corners, the design being the Garter Star, die stamped in brass.

The design on the buttons was the Garter Star with the motto 'Honi soit qui mal y pense' on the garter.

On the issue of percussion muskets about 1836 (the Guards were not fully armed with these until 1843) a small pocket was sewn into the coatee on the right side front just above the waist, for the percussion caps.

Fig 34: Two Privates in Marching Order, *c.* 1856

This photograph of an oil painting by the author depicts two Privates in Marching Order. The information on dress was from photographs of the period and an article and illustration that appeared in the Illustrated London News *of April 1856, describing the then new uniform of the Coldstream Guards.*

The head-dress has altered slightly in shape being smaller than before, still of course having the red plume on the right, and with a brass chin chain.

The double-breasted tunic of red cloth, had blue collar, epaulette straps and cuffs. The collar was piped over the top edge in white and had white embroidered Garter Stars on each side of the front. The epaulette straps were also piped in white round the edge and had a white embroidered heraldic Rose on the blue strap. The edge of the tunic was piped in white down the front. The brass buttons were arranged in pairs on each side, having eight pairs in each row and a single button at the top on the right side of the tunic. (The design on the buttons was the same as described for the officers in Fig 31 but now had a rim.) The cuffs had a blue flap on which were four loops in white lace in pairs with brass buttons on each, and white piping round the top of the blue cuff (in fact similar in all respects as the Full Dress cuffs of today). The pocket flaps on the skirts, I have shown as having the loops in pairs. It is reasonable to think that this would be the case but according to the illustration in the Illustrated London News *mentioned above, this is not the case; the skirts are shown with a pocket flap similar to the officers' type of 1810–15 on the Frock coatee, but the opposite way round, the buttons being on the outside and three in number. I am inclined to treat this rendering with some reserve, as there are in the general illustration, many mistakes that do not agree with the photographs of the period. It must be remembered that the artists had to work quickly and did not have any particular interest in the small details. This work was then copied by the wood engraver who made the blocks for publication; consequently many errors were made. I leave it to the reader to judge which is the correct information.*

Equipment is of whitened leather while the pouch-belt has lost the old brass buckles so long peculiar to the Guards. The pouch itself is black polished leather. The black valise now has the brass Garter Star badge. The bayonet is suspended in a frog from a waist-belt in a black scabbard with brass mounts. The brass clasp of the waist-belt has the Garter Star in the centre, and the ring around has the words 'Coldstream Guards' in fact the same as today. Haversacks are worn over the left shoulder as shown in photographs of the period. (In 1857 an order directed that the haversack was to be worn over the right shoulder.)

The water-bottle is the same as used in the Peninsular campaign. The trousers were of Oxford mixture with red stripes down outside seams. The men were armed with the 1855 pattern Enfield rifle. The mess-tin in black oilskin cover was attached to the grey greatcoat rolled on top of the valise.

Fig 35 : Private and Drummer, *c.* 1860

The dress detail for this drawing is from an old photograph showing the Coldstream Guards relieving an unknown Line regiment. As the Line regiment still wears the shako introduced in 1855 a modification of the old 'Albert' shako, it suggests the date to be around 1860.

The dress is very similar to the description given for Fig 34 but now the tunic is single-breasted, an alteration made in 1856. The dress is now more like that of the Coldstream Guards of today. The skirts were still rather long and full. The button arrangement was the same as today; four pairs and then one above the belt buckle. Another was under the buckle but this was a flat brass

one with no regimental distinction. Equipment was the same as described for 1856 in Fig 34. The pouch has the Garter Star badge again, and the men are in light marching order, the greatcoat is carried inside the valise and the grey-blue blanket on the outside, the mess-tin in oilskin cover on top. As long as muzzle loading weapons were used, the pouch-belt had a small pocket about breast high for the percussion caps. The drummer's tunic is laced in the well-known 'fleur-de-lis' of white and blue. The tunic was of scarlet cloth with blue collar, epaulette straps, wing shells and cuffs, all edged with lace, the wing shells being practically covered with this. A white embroidered Rose is on the blue epaulette strap and the collar and edge of the wings were fringed in blue and white. When the double-breasted tunic was introduced, the drummer's still remained single breasted, possible so as not to disturb the lace pattern on the breast of the tunic, this was as before; ten loops of lace in pairs, so their tunic was not affected by the alteration.

The trousers for both were of Oxford mixture, practically black, with red stripes down the outside seams.

Fig 36 : Drummer Boys, *c.* 1875

This delightful photograph of three small drummer boys of the Coldstream Guards gives a good idea of the dress of this particular period. Two wear the bearskin cap while the third has his forage cap on, which is of blue cloth with a plain white band and white piping round the crown, a brass Garter Star badge, the lower point of which just touches the white band. The bearskin caps have the red horse hair plume on the right, and brass chin chains. The tunics are of scarlet cloth, with blue collar, epaulette straps, wing shells and cuffs. The lace white with blue 'fleur-de-lis'. The collar and wings had blue and white fringes. On the epaulette strap a white embroidered Rose. All buttons were brass and the trousers have a red stripe down the outside seams. Drum carriages were whitened leather and leather drum aprons were worn. The boy on the left of the photograph holds a fife and laying in front of him is the bearskin cap belonging to the lad in the centre.

The drums have a blue painted front on which in full colour is the Royal Arms with labels, and the regimental motto, battalion and battle honours. The drum hoops are of the distinctive colouring of the Coldstream; a blue worm on a white ground and red edges. The blue and white striped ticken drum cover is tied on the side of the drum. The boy on the right holds a small terrier dog which is not very clear in the photograph.

Fig 36

Fig 37: Drummer and Fifer in Greatcoats

This line-drawing by the author shows what the boys would look like in their greatcoats. The material is of grey (blue/grey to be more precise) cloth, the cape being really part of the coat. Five brass regimental buttons are worn down the front with normal waist-belt and drum carriage.

Fig 38 : Drum Major, *c.* 1875

This photograph is of Drum Major Price. He wears the forage cap with the gold lace band, drooping peak edged with gold lace and Garter Star cap badge. The tunic is of scarlet cloth, with blue collar, wings and cuffs, all heavily laced in gold. The gold lace epaulette straps have a silver embroidered Rose with silver embroidered Garter Stars on the gold laced collar. Four large gold lace chevrons on a blue cloth patch are worn on each upper arm with a crimson sash over the right shoulder. The whitened leather waist-belt with slings carries a senior NCO's pattern sword and scabbard with brass mounts, gold cord sword knot and acorn. His trousers have the usual red stripe down the outside seam.

Fig 39 : Undress Uniforms, *c.* 1875

This photograph of a musketry instruction class shows an interesting group of all ranks in their undress uniforms. It shows us two ways of wearing the regulation side hat. Firstly, in the normal fore and aft fashion with the cap badge of the Garter Star on the left side near the front, six men in the group wear it this way. Five of the men wear it with the cap across the head and the side turned down as a peak, with the cap badge placed in the centre. The cap itself was of blue cloth wtih white piping. Ten of the men have a regimental pullover with alternative stripes across the body, and wear a neckerchief or scarf, the sergeants and corporals have their stripes on both arms in this dress. Varoius other forms of dress shown are:

A senior NCO in forage cap of blue cloth with a gold lace band, drooping peak edged in gold braid, and Garter Star badge, wearing his red serge tunic with blue collar and round cuffs. To the right a sergeant in white drill jacket with crimson sash, chevrons on both arms. In the centre, an officer in forage cap and blue patrol jacket, his trousers have wide scarlet stripes down the outside edge. (This dress is described fully in Fig 41.)

Fig 40: Officer in blue Frock uniform, Sergeant and Corporal in White Drill Jackets, *c.* 1875

This photograph shows an Officer and NCOs at signalling drill. The officer has the blue cloth forage cap with black braid band, drooping black patent

leather peak and chin strap. There is gold lace round the edge of the peak and a silver Garter Star with blue enamelled Garter and red cross in the centre of the cap. The blue frock with black mohair braid has six bars across the breast, four olivettes on each bar. On the collar, down the front edges of the coat, along the back seams to the waist with eyes and fringe at the waist and tassels on the back skirts is more mohair braiding. There is also figured braiding on the collar and cuffs. The trousers are dark blue with wide scarlet stripes down outside seam.

The sergeant and corporal both wear the forage cap of blue cloth; the sergeant has a gold lace band, while the corporal has white. Both have black patent leather chin straps. Both wear a brass Garter Star badge and they wear white drill jackets with eight brass buttons down the front and one on each cuff at the back, with chevrons worn on both arms. The trousers are blue/black with red stripes down the outside seams. The sergeant is a full rank, not a lance sergeant.

Fig 41 : Sergeant in white drill jacket and Officer in blue patrol jacket, *c.* 1878

This line-drawing gives a clearer picture of the dress of the Sergeant and Officer at this period. The sergeant's dress has been fully described in Fig 40. The officer's forage cap is as also described in Fig 40. The blue patrol jacket with black mohair braid has six bars across the breast, with our olivettes on each bar, the cuffs having the braid sewn round and coming to a point on the outside. The edge of the collar, down the front edges and round the skirts are also bound in braid, as well as along each pocket. The dark blue trousers have a wide scarlet stripe down the outside seams. In this dress, black leather anklets were worn at times.

The Drill Sergeant wears a forage cap of blue cloth with a gold lace band and piping round the crown. The drooping black patent leather peak has gold braid round the edge with the Garter Star badge above, the lower ray of which just touches the edge of the gold band.

The tunic was of scarlet cloth with a blue collar, epaulette straps, cuffs and cuff slashes. White piping was worn over the top of the collar and down the edge of the tunic, around the edge of the cuff slash and top of the cuffs and on the back skirt. Gold lace was worn round the top of the collar under the white piping with gold lace patches each side of the front of the collar. On the centre of these, on blue cloth backing were silver embroidered Garter Stars. The epaulette straps were edged with gold lace, a silver embroidered Rose on each strap. The cuff slashes were laced all round inside the white piping with a narrow flat gold lace leaving a blue 'light' between the white piping and the gold lace. Four gold lace loops in pairs were worn showing a strip of the blue cloth between the pairs with a brass button on each loop. There were two bands of gold lace round the top of the cuff under the white piping and gold lace loops in pairs on the skirt slashes, with gold lace edging. All buttons were brass. The drill sergeant is shown with a silver watch chain hanging down from the second button of the tunic; this was a common item of wear in this period. The rank chevrons of broad gold lace on blue backing, have the crimson colour badge with gold embroidered Crown, a crimson cap above, and silver embroidered scimitar bladed swords with gold hilts below. On the crimson colour a silver Garter Star with the Sphinx in silver underneath, this badge being worn on both arms. A crimson sash was worn over the right shoulder with a narrow white waist-belt with slings and Senior NCO's sword and scabbard, not seen in the illustration.

The Sergeant Major wears a forage cap similar in all respects to the drill sergeant, but has a wider gold lace round the peak.

The tunic was of similar quality in all respects to the drill sergeant, except that the sergeant-major had four broad gold lace chevrons on each arm with a gold and coloured embroidered Royal Arms on each. The sash, sword, etc, was as worn by the drill sergeant.

Fig 43: Privates in Valise Equipment, 1880

In the year 1875 the Valise Equipment was introduced and the drawing shows three different views of this as it was worn. It was of whitened buff leather, and consisted of a waist-belt (with a brass regimental clasp buckle), to which was attached, at the front and back, braces going over each shoulder. On each brace, at the front was a brass 'D' from which the black valise was suspended by two straps on each side. The top strap on each side had a brass buckle for adjustment. The valise hung over the small of the back, and in the centre the brass valise Garter Star was placed. On top of the valise, the mess-tin in oilskin cover was placed and secured by a strap. Attached to the top of the braces, through brass D rings were the straps securing the folded greatcoat, the loose ends of these being neatly rolled at the top. Tucked between the straps at the back was the 'fore and aft' forage cap. The cartridge pouches were placed on the front of the waist-belt secured each side of the belt clasp. The bayonet was suspended on the left side by a frog from the same belt. The haversack was worn over the right shoulder, underneath the equipment, the bag going under the left arm but over the bayonet scabbard. A small neat wooden water-bottle with whitened buff leather strap, was worn over the left shoulder.

This equipment was modified and improved in 1882, the valise being in-creased in size, the greatcoat carried under the flap and the mess-tin still being placed on top. Two larger collapsible cartridge pouches replaced the old box type. The strap of the water-bottle was removed, and this was now attached to the belt by a metal clip.

The men are all armed with the Martini-Henry rifle and triangular bayonet.

The dress of the privates at this period was the black bearskin cap with red horse hair plume on the right side and brass chin chain. Scarlet tunic (the other ranks' tunic was ordered to be of scarlet cloth in 1871) blue collar, epaulette straps, cuffs and cuff slashes. White piping ran over the collar down the front edge of the tunic, round the epaulette straps, cuff slashes, cuffs and back skirt. The collar had white worsted embroidered Garter Stars and a white worsted embroidered Rose on the epaulette straps. Four white worsted loops on the cuff slashes and back skirt slashes were set in pairs, a brass button on each loop, but not on the skirts, as these buttons were removed in 1875 because of the method of carrying the valise. The reason for this is obvious. The buttons were not replaced until 1904. The loops on the skirt slash were edged in blue cloth piping (see Fig 46 for detail). Nine brass buttons were worn on the front of the tunic in pairs and one single one over the belt buckle. The trousers were dark blue with the usual scarlet stripes.

Fig 44: Privates in Campaign Dress, Egypt, 1882, and the Sudan (Camel Corps), 1884

The figure on the left is in the uniform worn during the campaign in Egypt in 1882 against the rebels led by Arabi Pasha. The head-dress is a white helmet with puggaree worn with a red serge tunic, with plain dark blue collar and cuffs, there being no piping of any description on this tunic. The trousers were dark blue with a red stripe down the outside seams tucked into gaiters of black leather. The equipment worn was the valise pattern of 1875, in this case the private is shown in battle order; this was the braces and waist-belt with the two pouches, but in addition a black 'expense' pouch was attached to the waist-belt in the middle of the back. Suspended above this by straps from the 'Ds'

was the mess-tin in a black cover. All the buttons on this tunic were brass.

The figure on the right is in the dress worn by the Coldstream detachment of the Camel Corps. (The Regiment sent 92 of all ranks under Lieutenant-Colonel the Honourable E. Boscawen, Coldstream Guards). The head-dress is the usual white helmet with a jacket of a grey drab colour with brass buttons, buffish yellow breeches and dark blue puttees. The equipment consisted of a leather bandolier, the waist-belt and pouches of the 'improved Valise Equipment of 1882'. A canvas haversack and water-bottle of the clip-on type was also worn.

Both men are armed with the Martini-Henry rifle. The bayonet in 1882 was of the triangular pattern, while the Camel Corps had the long curved bayonet of the later type issued in 1883.

It is interesting to note that Gleichen's account of his experiences With the Camel Corps Up the Nile *(1888, Chapman Hall) in an extract writes: 'The Heavies and ourselves were dressed alike in grey serge jumpers and we amused ourselves by cutting out red cloth badges and letters to distinguish the various corps, 1GG (Gleichen was a Lieutenant in the 1st Grenadier Guards). These were sewn on the right arm.'*

It appears from the above account that the Guards' contingents of the Came Corps wore these identifications and possibly other regiments' detachments as well.

Fig 45: Officers of the 1st Battalion, *c.* 1890

This photograph gives the dress of junior officers at this period. The bearskin cap at this time for officers was more rounded and closely resembled that of the other ranks, later it was to become taller and narrower as we know it today. (The officer on the right seems to have his own idea how the bearskin should be groomed.) The plume for officers was of cut red feathers 6 inches long worn on the right with a brass tapered chin chain backed with black leather.

The tunic of superfine scarlet cloth, had a blue collar, cuffs, cuff flaps and shoulder straps. White piping ran over the top of the collar, down the front of the tunic, down the centre of the skirts and edge of the skirt flaps (see Fig 52 for details). Narrow gold lace ran round the top of the collar under the white piping, a gold lace patch on each side of the front, on this, a silver embroidered Garter Star. The shoulder straps were edged round in gold lace and fastened with a gilt regimental button. The cuff flap, had four gold lace loops on each and gilt regimental buttons, in pairs, with narrow gold lace round top of cuff under the white piping. The skirt flaps had gold lace loops in pairs with a button on each. The front of the tunic had nine regimental buttons and one plain that is covered by the waist-belt, eight of these buttons are in pairs and one single above the waist-belt clasp. A crimson sash was worn over the left shoulder with a white buff leather waist-belt with slings for the sword. The gilt buckle had a silver Garter Star and on the rim 'COLDSTREAM GUARDS'. which had the steel hilt pierced and chased in the guard with the Garter Star, a black fish-skin grip, bound with silver wire, in a steel scabbard. Trousers were of blue cloth with scarlet stripes 2 inches wide.

Field officers and captains had gold embroidery round the bottom of the collar and round the skirts and sleeve flaps and a second bar round the cuff. All this was in addition to the above description.

Fig 46 : Private and Drum Major in Marching Order, *c.* 1892

The Private in Marching Order wears the Slade-Wallace equipment introduced in 1888, its main characteristic being the valise carried high up on the shoulders, an improvement over the old Valise Equipment of 1875 and

1882. The black polished valise had the brass Garter Star badge in the centre with the flap secured by three black leather straps and brass buckles at the bottom. The valise itself was secured to the shoulder braces, through brass D rings. The greatcoat and blanket were nearly rolled and strapped, again through brass D rings, on the waist-belt. On top, in an oilskin cover was placed the mess-tin; this was secured by a strap going over the top of it, through a small leather runner sewn on the oilskin cover. All loose ends of the straps were neatly rolled through the buckles. On the front, each side of the waist-belt clasp, were attached two collapsible pouches, a small strap from underneath securing the flap. (Later the pouches were altered and reversed, so that the flap opened from inside.) On the front of the braces a narrower strap ran over the top, down to brass D rings. This was the strap that secured the valise and could also be adjusted to allow the valise to be removed without disturbing the rest of the equipment. On field training a small spade was carried, attached to the waist-belt by a frog, hanging down alongside the bayonet scabbard. A white canvas haversack was slung over the right shoulder, the strap of this had a brass runner for adjustment. Over the left shoulder, by a white buff leather strap, hung the round flat blue-grey cloth covered water-bottle.

This private was dressed in a black bearskin with red horse hair plume on the right side. A tunic of scarlet cloth with blue collar, shoulder straps, cuffs and cuff flaps or slashes with white piping over the top of the collar, down the front of the tunic, round the shoulder straps, edge of cuff flaps and round top of cuffs. There was also white piping down the centre between the skirt flaps to the hem. Cuff flaps had four loops in pairs on each, with a regimental button on each loop. The skirt flaps had four worsted loops in pairs on each flap, and were piped along the edges on the inside and bisecting the loops, with blue cloth. Nine buttons were worn down the front of the tunic, eight in pairs and a single above the belt clasp, this clasp of regimental design, the rim having 'COLDSTREAM GUARDS', and a Garter Star on the clasp. No buttons were worn on the skirt flaps, these were removed in 1875 and not replaced until 1904. See Fig 43 for details.

The Drum Major in Marching Order wears a red feather plume on the bearskin. A tunic of scarlet cloth, with blue collar, cuffs and cuff flaps. The tunic was heavily laced with narrow gold lace over the collar and down the front of the tunic, gold patches on the collar with silver embroidered Garter Stars. Eight bars of gold lace in pairs, with a brass regimental button on each were worn on the breast. The shoulder straps were of gold lace, with a silver embroidered Rose, the wing shells were of blue cloth with gold lace, so close that only narrow blue 'lights' showed with a gold fringe to the edge of the shell. The sleeves laced up each seam, back and front, with eight single gold lace inverted chevrons and double lace over the cuffs. The cuff flap was piped in white and narrow gold lace with four loops in pairs of gold lace with a brass regimental button on each. Four large gold lace chevrons were worn on the right arm, points up, on blue cloth backing. The back of the tunic was laced on the seams, the skirt slashes in similar quality to the first-class tunic. (See Fig 47.) A crimson sash was worn over the right shoulder with a white buff leather waist-belt with regimental clasp, white sword slings and a steel scabbard to the sword.

The drum major is shown as he would appear on field days or drill. The embroidered sash was not worn, and a short cane replaced the drum major's staff.

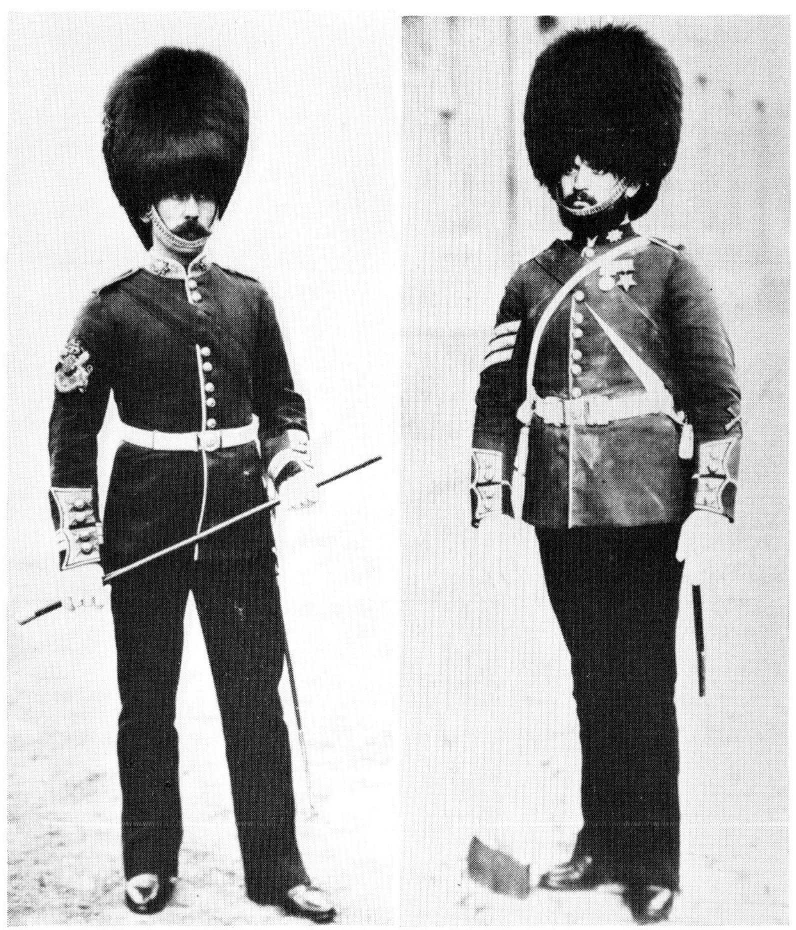

*The black bearskin cap had the plume of red cut feathers (all senior NCOs
from the rank of full sergeant upwards wore this plume). The tunic of the
RSM was of first-class quality scarlet cloth with blue collar, shoulder straps,
cuffs and cuff flaps. White piping ran over the top of the collar, the front of
the tunic, round the edge of each cuff flap and round the top of the cuffs also
from between the waist buttons at the back, down to the edge of the skirt.
Flat gold lace was worn round the top of the collar under the white piping
with gold lace patches on the front of the collar and silver embroidered Garter
Stars on blue backing. Shoulder straps were edged with gold tracing braid
and a silver embroidered Rose on the strap. Cuff flaps were edged with gold
lace alongside the white piping, leaving a blue light between. Four gold lace
loops in pairs were worn each with a brass regimental button and gold lace
loops on the skirts in pairs. The embroidered Royal Arms was worn on the
right arm only. (The wearing of badges of rank for all NCOs on the right arm
only, probably dates from about 1883.) A crimson sash was worn over*

the right shoulder with a white buff waist-belt and sword slings suspending a senior NCO's sword and scabbard. The trousers were of dark blue cloth with narrow red stripes. The pioneer sergeant's bearskin was as for the RSM in Fig 47, worn with a scarlet tunic of sergeant's quality with blue collar, shoulder straps, cuffs and cuff flaps. White piping was as for the RSM, except that the tunic of sergeant's quality had the shoulder straps piped in white. Gold lace loops in pairs on the cuff flaps and skirt flaps were worn, there being a regimental button on each loop of the cuff flaps, but no buttons on the skirts (see Fig 46), the edge of the skirt flaps were piped in blue cloth. Chevrons were in gold lace on a blue backing, with crossed gold embroidered axes with silver Rose above. The sergeant has the musketry proficiency badge on his lower arm left, on a blue backing. A crimson sash was worn over the right shoulder and he also has a water-bottle strap over the left shoulder and a haversack over the right, this is folded and over the pioneer's sword in a black scabbard.

Fig 48: Pioneer and Private of the Regimental Transport, *c.* 1896

The Pioneer in Marching Order wears a black bearskin with a red horse hair plume and tapered brass chin chain. The tunic was of scarlet cloth, with blue collar, shoulder straps, cuffs and cuff flaps. White piping ran over the top of the collar, down the front of the tunic, around the shoulder straps, round the edge of the cuff flaps, along the top of the cuffs and the centre of the skirt flaps down to the hem of the skirt. White worsted embroidered Garter Stars were worn on the collar with a white embroidered Rose on the shoulder strap. Cuff flaps had four worsted loops in pairs on each flap with a brass button on each loop. The skirt flaps (or slashes), had four worsted loops on each flap in pairs, with no buttons. Nine brass buttons were worn down the front of the tunic, eight in pairs and one single above the belt buckle. On the right arm, crossed axes in white, with Rose above. Normal Slade-Wallace belt and braces, valise etc, but no cartridge pouches, instead a variety of pouches and wallets for tools. A Pioneer's sword with a saw back was worn in a black scabbard with steel tip. Dark blue trousers with red stripes on outer seams were worn over black gaiters and boots.

The Private of the Regimental Transport in Marching Order wears a bearskin and tunic, similar to the Pioneer. but without the Pioneer trade badge on the right arm. The equipment consists of the waist-belt, haversack and water-bottle with the addition of a whip. Bedford cord breeches of a buffish grey colour were worn. Puttees are blue with steel spurs. On the right leg, secured by three straps and brass buckles, is the 'leg iron' to protect the leg of the driver when in pole draught, ride and drive.

Drum Major Patrick, 2nd Bn. See Fig 49 for more details.

Fig 49 : Drum Major Patrick of
the 2nd Battalion in Full Dress,
c. 1898

*The description of the Drum
Major's dress is the same as that
described in Fig 46 except that
here he wears the Drum Major's
sash of blue with two gold laces
and a blue 'light' in between that
went around both edges and a
gold fringe at the bottom. On each
side of the front was a drumstick
held in place by gold loops, between
these a gold embroidered Crown
with a crimson cap and white base,
below this the Garter Star in silver
embroidery with coloured garter
and cross. Gold embroidered foliage
and labels with blue centres, carried
the battle honours in gold thread.
In the centre of this was a silver
embroidered Sphinx badge. In his
right hand the drum major's staff
of gold and silver regimental
devices chased into the design.*

Fig 50 : Group of the 3rd Battalion, *c.* 1898

*This interesting photograph of the 3rd Battalion is mainly of officers, one of
them, on the extreme left, gives us the back view of his dress. He is a junior*

officer and as the parade is evidently a state occasion he and all the officers wear their gold and crimson sashes and gold lace waist-belts and slings, all lined with crimson morocco leather. The back skirt flaps or slashes are well shown; two 3-pointed flaps piped in white with a single white piping between from waist to the skirt. Gold lace loops were in pairs with gilt buttons of regimental design on each. (Field officers and captains would have an extra gold lace edging on the inside of the white piping on the flaps of the skirts.)

Three other ranks are shown, a sergeant piling arms, and two privates, one of whom gives a back view. He is in review order, having his waist-belt, and one cartridge pouch fastened in the middle of the back, beside the bayonet frog. His skirt flaps in white worsted loops have no buttons (see Fig 43 for more details).

In 1897 Parliament sanctioned the addition of a 3rd Battalion to the Regiment. The Colours were presented by the Queen at Aldershot in July 1898.

Fig 51 : The Boer War — Privates in Campaign Dress, 1899 and 1900

The figure on the right shows the dress that the Coldstream wore in the first year of the Boer War. It consisted of the helmet with puggaree over which was a khaki cover; a khaki jacket with patch pockets with flaps on the breast, five brass buttons down the front, two small buttons fastening the shoulder straps and two on the breast pockets, khaki trousers and puttees. The equipment was the Slade-Wallace but without the valise, in place of this the haversack was worn thrown over the shoulders to hang square on the shoulder blades. The greatcoat and blanket was carried in a roll in the middle of the back, fastened by straps to the D rings on the waist-belt. On top of this was the mess-tin secured by a strap.

A red plume may have been worn for a short time with the helmet, as on October 20 1899 the 2nd Battalion and reservists were inspected before their departure for South Africa by HRH The Duke of Cambridge and Major-General H. Trotter, Commander Home District. The battalion paraded in helmets, with red serge frocks and home service trousers, a small red plume, supplied by regimental funds, was worn in the helmet. Officers wore in addition small Garter Star badge.

The figure on the left shows the dress after July 1900 when the old pattern pouches and helmets were discarded and in their place the bandolier equipment and felt hats were issued to both battalions then serving in the campaign. The felt hat in the Coldstream was worn turned up on the right side with a red plume and small Garter Star badge.

Both figures are armed with the Lee Enfield rifle, the same as the Lee-Metford of 1888 but having the Enfield modified barrel.

Fig 52: Regimental Quartermaster, *c.* 1904

The dress of the Regimental Quartermaster was the same in all respects as the Regimental Officers. The Quartermaster in the photograph has two stars of the Order of the Bath in embroidery on his shoulder straps. (The Guards badges of rank, at this time, followed the rest of the Army, it was not until 1920 that the Coldstream had the Garter Star as rank badges.) The sash was now worn round the waist (this was ordered for the Army about 1902). The striking difference in dress of the RQM was the cocked hat of black felt, with a loop of one inch gold lace over a black silk cockade, secured by a gilt regimental button, from this a plume of red swan feathers, five inches high.

Before the alteration of the position of the sash from the left shoulder to the waist; the RQM wore a black sword-belt with a regimental clasp.

Fig 53: A Group of Coldstreamers, *c.* 1902

This picture shows two Privates, a Pioneer Corporal and a Drummer, all in

full marching order. The dress of each has been described in detail elsewhere, but this photograph is of interest as it shows the pouches of the privates in the reverse position, so that the flap opens from the inside. It also shows us alternative articles of equipment as carried by the pioneers, and lastly, a drummer in full marching order.

Fig 54: Drummer, Corps of Drums, *c.* 1904.

The drummer wears the 'Broderick' cap introduced in about 1902. It was of blue cloth with white piping round the welt, a white band, and a brass Garter Star cap badge. The tunic is of scarlet cloth, with blue collar, shoulder straps, wing shells, cuffs and cuff flaps. The lace is white with blue 'fleur-de-lis' and was in two thicknesses; narrow lace over the top of the collar, around shoulder straps and wing shells. The wider lace on the breast in ten double lace loops in pairs, down the sleeve seams and seven chevrons, points up, on each arm. The back of the tunic was laced on each seam down to the hem of the skirt with a short length of lace from the back of the shoulders up to the collar. The skirt flaps were three pointed and edged in blue cloth piping, with four lace loops on each flap in pairs. The collar had a blue and white fringe, also the edge of the wings. The cuff flaps were piped in white with four lace loops in pairs on each. Nine brass regimental buttons ran down the front of the tunic, eight in pairs and one single above the belt clasp. In addition there was one more button on each shoulder strap, cuff flap lace loops, and the skirt flaps (these latter were replaced in this year 1904). On the shoulder strap was an embroidered Rose. White waist-belt had a regimental clasp, a fife case on the right side, normal issue bayonet, in frog, on the left. (The Drummers' sword was officially withdrawn about this time.) Dark blue trousers had scarlet stripes.

Fig 55: Massed Bands at Practice, Chelsea Barracks, *c.* 1910

This photograph of the massed bands is interesting because it shows the forage cap that followed the 'Broderick'. Now a peak with a brass binding has been added. At first the top was completely flat, with no cap badge, but shortly after the front was raised and the cap badge added, as can be seen in this photograph. This peaked forage cap was first issued to the Coldstream in 1908. In the fore-

ground on the left are two side drummers of the military band, next to them is a bandsman, then the military band Time Beater. All four have gold lace service chevrons on the left arm, their tunics are all laced in gold, with gold wings with a fringe. Behind these are the Corps of Drums, some in their full dress tunics, the rest are in white drill jackets. The service stripes on the tunics for the Corps of Drums were white worsted on blue backing. Owing to the drummers lace chevrons having points up, the service stripes for all bandsmen and drummers were worn point down. All other ranks have them points up. See the military bandsman on left in photograph.

The rehearsal could have been for the Guards' Tattoo that took place about this time, or for the Trooping the Colour.

Fig 56: Parade of Orderly NCOs, Chelsea Barracks, *c.* 1906

Here we see the daily parade of the company orderly NCOs at BHQ. The front rank consists of Lance and Full Sergeants. Lance sergeants do not wear a sash and their tunic is the same in all respects as the private, except for three white chevrons on blue backing on the right arm. In rank, they are the equivalent to a corporal, full corporal that is in the rest of the Army. A Guards' corporal's rank is the same as a lance corporal in the Army.

Behind the sergeants are the Orderly Corporals, and behind them, the Battalion Orderly Sergeant, in this case a colour sergeant. They are all in Greatcoat Order, the chevrons on the lower right arm, are of blue cloth on scarlet backing. The Colour Sergeant has a blue crown on scarlet backing above his chevrons. The colour of the coat is blue/grey. It will be noted that gaiters were still being worn (they were not officially abolished until Army Order 293 of 1920). All carry regimental canes.

Fig 57 : Parade of the 3rd Battalion at Wellington Barracks, 1906

This photograph of the parade of the 3rd Battalion before their departure to Egypt is interesting as it shows the battalion with their foreign service Wolseley helmets, with the red horse hair plume for the men and red feather hackle for the officers and senior NCOs. Officers have a spike on their helmets and a Garter Star badge in front on the puggari, unlike the other ranks who have plain helmets.

The equipment shown is that of 1903 called the Bandolier Equipment which had no valise; instead the greatcoat was folded and placed up on the shoulders (similar to the method used with the old 1875 Valise Equipment of carrying the greatcoat). The mess-tin was attached to the waist-belt, below the coat. The waist-belt had five small pouches each holding two clips of five rounds. A leather bandolier over the left shoulder held a further 50 rounds. The bayonet was suspended from a frog on the left side, and a haversack was slung over the right shoulder. A water-bottle, of oblong shape covered in grey felt in a web carriage was carried under the right arm.

Fig 58 : Guard Order, 1912

Here we see the Full Dress Guard Order. The wearing of the valise was discontinued in November 1905, and the folded greatcoat was worn instead, the Valise Star was placed on the centre strap. On the right of the front rank, stands the Company Orderly Sergeant, in this case, a Lance Sergeant. His tunic was the same as the Private's, but with the addition of three plain white stripes on blue backing, and he wears no sash (only full sergeants and above wearing the sash.)

The Guard are armed with the Short Magazine Lee Enfield, this was introduced about 1902 (this was a shortened version of the Lee Enfield, brought in to be suitable for both infantry and cavalry). A long bayonet was issued with

Fig 59 : Privates in Service Dress, 1914–1918

As we have seen, several types of drab service dress had been worn during
the various campaigns up to the Boer War, when the value of this variety of
dress was finally apparent to the authorities. So in January 1902 an Army Order
introduced a universal service dress for wear on most occasions when full
dress was not worn. This was the form with slight modifications, that was to be
worn right up to the outbreak of the 1939–45 war, when battledress was
adopted.

The service dress of khaki drab was at first rather loose fitting tunic with
patch pockets on the breast and pockets with flaps sewn in the lining on the
hips, brass buttons of universal pattern, five large down the front of the tunic,
and one small one fastening the shoulder straps and each pocket flap Trousers
of the same material and puttees completed the dress. At first a 'Broderick'
cap was worn but in 1905 a khaki peaked cap replaced this. The dress was
gradually tailored and smartened over the years, until it became as seen on the
Corporal in the last colour plate.

In 1908 the web equipment as shown in the drawing replaced the bandolier
type of 1903. This new pattern service equipment was made of webbing, it had

five small pouches on each side of a broad waist-belt, these pouches each held ten rounds in clips of five ·303 inch ammunition. The valise was attached to the shoulder straps or braces by a brass buckle on each side. The haversack was suspended from the left side by two webbing tabs, one on the back of the waist-belt, the other from under the pouches. The water-bottle was suspended in a similar fashion on the right side. The entrenching tool was carried suspended from the waist-belt over the buttocks, and the entrenching tool handle was strapped alongside the bayonet scabbard. The water-bottle was metal enamelled and covered with khaki cloth or felt material. The figure on the right, in marching order 1914 is wearing the equipment in the fashion described above.

The figure on the left is in fighting order 1916 and wears the steel helmet issued in this year. A gas mask was worn in the 'Alert' position on the chest. The haversack is worn up on the back with the mess-tin in a khaki cover.

Both men are armed with the SMLE Rifle issued around 1902 with the long bayonet.

During the war formation signs were worn both on the helmet and sleeves of the tunic. The brass Rose and CG were worn on the shoulder straps 1914–15, but these disappeared and in their place cloth numerals were worn.

Fig 61

Fig 60: Officers with the Colours, *c.* 1922 (opposite top)

This photograph is possibly of the Colours of the 1st and 2nd Battalions of the Regiment, as the 3rd was abroad at this time in the Army of the Black Sea at Constantinople.

The interesting point about this particular photograph is the tunics worn by four of the officers. After the Great War of 1914-1918, there was no immediate return to Full Dress, but in 1920 it was finally authorized. The first regiment to wear it in the Brigade, was a Guard of Honour of the Scots Guards in Edinburgh, July 1920, and the Scots Guards were the first to wear it for King's Guard in October of the same year.

The War Office whilst authorizing the return to Full Dress, sought to reduce much of the splendour, and amongst some of the economies set out, (ie abolishing the white drill jacket for the other ranks; the red serge tunic for warrant officers and staff sergeants and the black anklets for marching order, etc). It directed that the gold lace embroidery on the collar, cuffs and skirts of the officer's tunics, to be reduced, this was known as 'skeleton' lace, and this photograph shows four of the officers wearing it. It was so unpopular that in August 1925 it was abolished, and only a few tunics of this type were made. (In the photograph, the second officer from the left, with a Regimental Colour, has a pre-war tunic so comparison can easily be made between the two types of tunics.)

Fig 61 : Guard Order, pre-1936 and after, until 1939

On the right in the drawing is shown the pre-1936 'Guard Order' with the folded grey greatcoat, attached to the braces of the Slade-Wallace equipment by three white buff leather straps, the brass Valise Star was attached to the centre strap, the loose end of which was neatly rolled through the buckle at the bottom. The grey cloth cape was rolled and attached by two white buff leather straps, through the D rings of the waist-belt, the loose ends of the straps neatly rolled through the buckles on top. (The dress and equipment was exactly the same as that shown in Fig 59.)

On the left is shown the Guard Order as ordered in October 1936, one of the changes made by King Edward VIII during his short reign. Folded capes 14 inches by $6\frac{1}{2}$ inches with three folds, secured by three buff leather straps, the Valise Star fastened in the middle of the centre one, replaced the greatcoat. The top of the cape now being worn level with the piping on the top of the collar. (In greatcoat order, the cape was worn in the same fashion.)

The ends of the braces were rolled through the buckle just above the top of the waist belt. Pouches were later laid aside, the waist-belt and braces only being worn, with the bayonet frog, in this order.

Fig 62: Coldstream Guards, World War 2, 1939–45

On the left is a Guardsman of the 3rd Battalion in Egypt 1942, in Fighting Order: the steel helmet covered in sacking; khaki drill shirt and shorts; khaki woollen hose tops and short puttees; 1937 pattern equipment. This equipment replaced the old 1908 pattern web; it consisted of a narrower waist-belt with braces and a large pouch on each side of the front, to which the braces were attached by brass D rings, these were then clipped at the back to two brass buckles sewn to the top of the waist-belt. The large pouches were so designed to carry full magazines for the Bren Light Machine Gun. The haversack or small pack, in Fighting Order was worn up on the back, suspended there by means of the valise straps. The water-bottle was carried inside the haversack alongside the square mess-tin in special compartments. The bayonet was carried in a frog on the left side, and the entrenching tool kit was suspended from the ends of the braces at the back by brass buckles. The field dressing was carried in a small pocket on the right side at the front (just below the waist-belt) of the shorts. The battalion was armed with the SMLE and long bayonet. The shorts could be turned down over the knees as a protection against mosquitos. A tape ran through the edge of the bottom of the leg of the shorts which was pulled tight, giving the appearance of a pair of bloomers. Needless to say these shorts proved to be very unpopular, and were soon altered.

Over each shoulder the Guardsman has a bandolier of canvas material with spare ammunition as drawn from the ammunition box.

The Corporal of the 2nd Battalion is shown in Full Marching Order at home 1942. Head-dress is the Soft Field Service Cap with stitched peak; khaki battledress blouse and trousers. On each shoulder was a red strip lettered white, COLDSTREAM GUARDS, below this two strips of red cloth denoting the battalion. The stripes of khaki with white centres were on both arms. The equipment worn is the 1937 pattern web as described above, but in this order the valise is shown with the steel helmet strapped on the back, on top of this is the brown and green gas cape secured by white tapes. The haversack (small pack) is suspended on the left side over the bayonet scabbard. A water-bottle is on the right and the entrenching tool kit is attached to the brace straps over the buttocks. The gas mask in khaki bag carried in the 'Alert' position on the breast above the two Bren pouches. Web gaiters were worn. The corporal is armed with the Mk IV rifle and short round bayonet, which was replacing the SMLE Rifle and long bayonet.

During the war the several battalions of the Coldstream would be wearing many different identification and brigade divisional signs etc. It is not possible in this book to go into these, as this is, itself, a specialist subject covered in other books.

Fig 63: Captain and Adjutant in Service Dress, 1965
Fig 64: Sergeant, Drill Order, Aden 1965

The Captain wears the blue cloth forage cap with black braid band and patent leather peak with gold lace round the edge and silver and enamel Garter Star badge on the front. The service dress jacket, of Guards pattern, of a brownish khaki colour with patch pockets on the breast and hips. The breast pockets have no pleat. Brass regimental buttons, six in pairs run down the front of *the jacket, two fastening the breast pocket flaps and two fastening the shoulder straps. On the shoulder straps each side a three Garter Star rank badges in brass.*

Breeches are grey, with grips blancoed in a red brick colour, boots are brown with yellow metal spurs. A Sam Browne belt is worn with frog for the sword with a scabbard of brown leather. The steel hilt of the sword is of regimental pattern. Brown leather covered cane and gloves complete this dress. The Sergeant wears the forage cap of blue cloth, piped white round the welt and band with a patent leather peak with brass binding round edge, and for sergeants two narrower bindings above. A khaki drill bush shirt with lower pockets removed and tucked in the khaki drill shorts. Normal pattern khaki stripes on right arm only. Red worsted sash; 1937 pattern web waist-belt, bayonet frog and rifle sling blancoed white. Woollen khaki hose tops with coloured bands round the turn over, blue/red/blue. Short khaki puttees. Self Loading Rifle and short bayonet.

Fig 65 : Sergeant and Guardsman, 2nd Battalion, No. 2 Dress, 1970

The Sergeant and Guardsman wear the forage cap of blue cloth with white piped welt and white band with the brass cap star, patent leather peak bound with brass rim; the sergeant has two extra brass bindings above this. The tunic and trousers are of a superfine greenish khaki material. Four brass buttons of regimental pattern are worn down the front with two more fastening the pocket flaps on the breast and shoulder straps. On the shoulder straps are a brass Rose and CG. The Sergeant has stripes on both arms and a red worsted sash, and white buff waist-belt and bayonet frog with brass clasp buckle of regimental pattern. The arms are the SLR and short bayonet.

Small red cloth strips, two in number are worn at the top of each sleeve to denote the battalion number.

This is the Fighting Order of today. The Guardsman's head-dress is the brown (khaki) beret. Disrupted pattern combat jacket and trousers are of grey/green/brown and black colouring. Dark green/grey is the colour of the 1958 pattern web equipment with all buckles and metal parts blued steel. The braces are much wider than the old pattern over the shoulders. Two pouches similar in size to the old Bren pouch are attached to the braces and waist belt in front. There is a frog at the side of the left hand pouch for the bayonet. Attached to the belt and braces at the back are two larger pouches that carry the mess-tin, waterbottle, rations and personal kit. When the respirator is worn at the 'Alert' position it is carried in front attached to the waist-belt between the two ammunition pouches, but on other occasions it is carried between the 'kidney' pouches.

Over the left shoulder is carried a belt of rimless 7.62 mm ammunition for the GPMG. Short khaki puttees, SLR and short bayonet, are also shown.

Fig. 68: Coldstream Guardsman, Northern Ireland, 1972

This picture shows a variation on the active service dress shown in Fig 67, with additional equipment worn while serving as 'Aid to the Civil Power'. For anti-riot work and street patrol the 'Flak Jacket' is worn over the combat dress jacket, and the steel helmet has a hinged transparent visor. The weapon shown is the so-called 'Elephant Gun' used for firing rubber bullets during riot control operations.